In Case of Loss

In Case of Loss

Lutz Seiler

*Translated from the
German by Martyn Crucefix*

SHEFFIELD - LONDON - NEW YORK

First published in English in 2023 by And Other Stories
Sheffield – London – New York
www.andotherstories.org

Originally published in German in the following books, for which copyright is as follows:
Sonntags dachte ich an Gott, © Suhrkamp Verlag Frankfurt am Main 2004.
Die Anrufung, © Lutz Seiler 2005
Am Kap des guten Abends, ©Insel Verlag Berlin 2018
Laubsäge und Scheinbrücke, © Lutz Seiler 2020

For details of the source publications of the German texts of the essays and non-fiction
pieces collected in *In Case of Loss*, please consult the Editorial Note after the texts.

1 3 5 7 9 8 6 4 2

Print ISBN: 9781913505783
eBook ISBN: 9781913505790

Editor: Stefan Tobler; Copy-editor: Robina Pelham Burn; Proofreader: Madeleine Rogers;
Typesetter: Tetragon, London; Typefaces: Albertan Pro and Linotype Syntax (interior)
and Stellage (cover); Series Cover Design: Elisa von Randow, Alles Blau Studio,
Brazil, after a concept by And Other Stories; Author Photo: Heike Steinweg.

And Other Stories books are printed and bound in the UK on FSC-
certified paper by Clays Ltd. The covers are of G . F Smith 270gsm Colorplan
card, which is sustainably manufactured at the James Cropper paper mill
in the Lake District, and are stamped with biodegradable foil.

And Other Stories gratefully acknowledges that its work is supported
using public funding by Arts Council England and the translation of
this book was supported by a grant from the Goethe-Institut.

CONTENTS

Under the Pine Vault   7

Huchel and the Dummy Bridge   29

'The post-war era never ends': On Jürgen Becker   34

In Case of Loss   49

Aurora: An attempt to answer the question
     'Where is the poem going today?'   66

Illegal Exit, Gera (East)   78

The Tired Territory   86

Babelsberg: Brief Thoughts on Ernst Meister   109

In the Anchor Jar   113

Sundays I Thought of God   121

The Flute Player   137

The Invocation   140

In the Movie Bunker   149

The Soggy Hems of His Soviet Trousers:
     Image as a way into the narration of the past   163

Notes   179

Editorial Note   181

UNDER THE PINE VAULT

1.

The house stands on the western edge of the village. The woods begin on a level with the house, the garden extending into the woods to be completely surrounded by the woods. Guests, stepping out of the house onto the terrace, exclaim, 'Oh, there isn't even a fence here.' The fence is deep in the forest, invisible. Coming south down the narrow, paved road, you have the impression of heading straight towards the house, then the road changes direction. To begin with, I did not notice that the property lies in a depression. The snow lingers here for so long, even in a time of thaw, that it is hard to believe it is snow and you feel the need to step outside and check.

Before work every morning, I walk around outside the house. I look at the bark on a pine tree or at a patch of grass. I stand beside the garage, or I gaze back towards the house from the rear, from the margins of the forest, and I am hardly present. With its pointed roof and square base, the house resembles a pyramid. The tall pine trees stretch above it; they dominate it. When the wind blows, the branches beat on the roof beneath which we sleep. On those occasions, we do not get much rest and we lie there thinking it is about time the forest was taken in hand. The pine trees form a vault that seems to close over the house at night. Francis

Ponge once described a pine forest as a 'factory of dead wood'. The branches that wither on the tall trees, then break off, lie scattered like dark limbs about the garden. I collect them up and pile them in the corner of our woodland plot. For a long time, this was all the gardening I ever did.

Last winter, one of the branches that had blown off in a storm crashed through the roof of the bicycle shed which stands near the *writing shed*. In the writing shed are kept all those things that have not managed to find a place in the house: books, a suitcase of letters, photographs, discarded toys, a terrarium with two shrivelled-up blindworms, plus other bits and pieces, including a desk. On the shelves, there are manuscripts and, for reasons I have never really explained to myself, my notes from university lectures on topics such as 'Aspects of Indus Culture' or 'History of the German-Italian Crusades'. I thought, perhaps, there would be something in them I might find useful. What that will be, only time can tell. Sometimes I stand there, in the shed, taking a look at something, though as if from a distance, the way I stand looking back at the house from the edge of the forest, or the way I stare at the bark of a tree. What is familiar enables me to absent myself. It is then things begin to come to mind.

2.

Beside the writing shed is the oldest of the three sheds, the *ur-shed*, the others being additions from later periods. The poet Peter Huchel used this as his cats' quarters, but also for tools and for parts of his *Sinn und Form* journal archive, which included correspondence and submitted work. The cat flap in the shed door is broken. Apart from a few stray items, the archive vanished after the death of the poet Erich Arendt, who lived in this house on

Hubertusweg after Huchel. It is said that Arendt never once set foot in Huchel's tool shed. He was not a man much interested in tools and not especially drawn to the idea of life in a rural setting. But Huchel was, and this was, in part, to sustain a closeness to the materials and matters of village life, and it was from his memory of these things that much of his writing arose. In a radio programme in 1932, Huchel followed St Augustine in laying claim to that 'great estate of memory, where heaven, earth and sea are present'. Huchel wrote in 1963 (in a letter of thanks to the West Berlin Academy, which had just awarded him the Fontane Prize) that the fact it turned out to be an estate in Brandenburg did not make it any less broad or limitless. Others, such as William Faulkner, Seamus Heaney and Les Murray, have also later moved back to the land which had already been cultivated in their writing. When Huchel bought the house and garden on Hubertusweg in the early 1950s, he had long sacralised the land, a process which, according to Joseph Campbell, is about recognising mythic symbols in the forms of the local landscape. Bertolt Brecht, who acted as real estate consultant on the purchase of the property, advised not paying any more than 6,000 marks for it. In the end, the purchase price was four times as much.

Firewood used to be cut in front of the shed: 'Looking up from the chopping-block / under a light rain, / with axe in hand . . .' The woodyard is bordered on the garden side by a couple of felled robinias, the so-called 'sitting logs', the best place to pass the time out of doors. Though a small table had been set up – nailed to a fallen acacia at the far end, closest to the forest – to let the poet work outside undisturbed, it is said he only rarely used it. At the time, the tool shed abutted another flimsy wooden shed and a sturdy fence behind which horses or sheep could be kept, something that was perhaps done in the pre-war years when the land still belonged to the novelist and scholar Bernhard Hoeft. But in Huchel's time, the gate would stand wide open and the fenced area was used as a coal store. Last summer, my son found 'black stones with writing on them' as he was digging in the garden, and he proudly filled his rucksack with these treasures. Buried beneath the sand, from the era of the coal store, there are still coal briquettes bearing the fragmentary lettering of the REKORD brand.

3.

In 1993 we moved from Berlin to Wilhelmshorst, initially to a house at the other end of the village. I hardly knew anything of the circumstances in which Huchel had lived in Wilhelmshorst. The sandy soil on the paths around the house and the pine trees spoke of 'the North' to me. When we used to go on holiday from Thuringia to the Baltic Sea, the coastal region began for us in this area and beyond it lay the sea.

As an initial image of our new home, *Cape Cod Evening* by Edward Hopper seemed about right. Hopper owned a house in Truro, on the North American Atlantic coast. The picture, painted in 1939, shows a man sitting on the steps of a house and a woman standing beside him, leaning against the wall. A dog, in tall, browning grass, is looking for something the man has thrown, or perhaps has yet to throw. The gesture the man is making with his hand is not clear; perhaps he is just brushing the tips of the grass, while the woman, whose dress is dark like the forest beyond the house, is gazing towards the dog. The forest behind the house did not remind me of our forest, yet the image still reminded me of our new home, of a kind of easeful absence that I recognised in the man and that gesture he is making by reaching out his hand. That attentive, abstracted look, which can bring poems into being, turned 'Cape Cod' into 'Cape Good' and that became 'good evening Cape', the title of the first poem I wrote while living 'out' in Wilhelmshorst. In this unfamiliar Brandenburg landscape, among people who were strangers to me and who did not greet each other on the street, I was able to write in a way that I had never managed in the city. I felt at home from the very first day. My short poem ends, as the daylight is fading off the tops of the trees, with the strange utterance of a dog, or more precisely the shadow of a dog, standing at the gate, saying: 'out here, I'm loved, you know, I'm loved'.

In Hopper's work, the individual brushstrokes remain visible, though they subordinate themselves to the overall impact of the image and what it intends to convey. An ideal model for a poem: every one of the means used is to be taken to the limits of perceptibility, where it remains visible and invisible at the same time and, without imposing itself, contributes to the story the poem wants to tell.

4.

On 8 October 1995, I wrote in my notebook: 'Broke into Huchel.' There had been difficulties with the local housing authorities, who worked from a couple of dilapidated buildings on the outskirts of Beelitz and had refused to hand over the keys to the house. Beside the house, in the sand, lay a corrugated-iron sheet. Beneath this was the opening to the coal bunker through which we gained access to the cellar and from there into a bathroom with flower-patterned tiles. A dead pine marten lay in the basement bathtub covered in coal dust. Peter Huchel's widow, Monica Huchel, who had, from a distance, instigated and legitimised this break-in, later explained over the phone how to work the National Boiler in the basement: a cast-iron marvel that not only required coal but coke as well, for which coal merchants in the 1950s had to be bribed. Back then, under cover of darkness, the black consignments would be dropped at the gate or lugged to the coal-hole: 'from their filthy baskets they pour / the lumpen black grief / of earth into my cellar'. Huchel called verses like this 'occasional poems' in the Goethean sense. He wrote directly from the things that surrounded him. These were the objects of the house, the garden, the everyday and, above all, the landscape. There is no doubt, the poems go far beyond the visible and the concrete but, for their author, it remained important that they were firmly 'of the earth'.

Before we broke open the front door from the inside, I wandered round the locked house for a while. The bathroom was the former laundry room for the 'maid', who until 1957 lived in a room between the kitchen and the dining room. Wastewater and sewage were pumped from the cellar out along a pipe into the pines. The cellar stairs led up to the kitchen and, from there, a small hallway led into the 'vestibule', as Monica Huchel called the hallway. From this vestibule, doors led off into the dining room and the 'editorial office', and from the centre of it the large, dark-stained staircase swept upwards. Also in the vestibule stood the 'classics shelf', in front of which Huchel once had his picture taken. In the photograph, you can see editions of the works of Chekhov, Schiller and Hauptmann, and, above them, sits a volume by Hermann Brockhaus which has holes in its spine; in its previous location, in Berlin, it had been damaged by shrapnel.

It actually felt colder inside the house than out, my breath condensing. I was sure there would be too many voices in this place. Too many, at any rate, for someone who tends to talk to himself, to the room at large, while engaged in writing. As I listened to the sound of my own footsteps through the vacant rooms, I was sure I ought to be treading and speaking more softly. As if the sound coming off the linoleum nailed onto the floorboards would be enough to dislodge from the walls the voices of previous inhabitants. Though that is not exactly what I wrote in my notebook on that first inspection of the house. There it says simply: 'replace heating, refurbish doors, wiring, windows, etc'.

5.

The garden – basically a clearing covered with forest grass, hemmed in and half roofed over by the surrounding pine trees – has a remarkable feature that only became visible to us in the spring, when we had already been living in the house on Hubertusweg for six months. In the back third of the garden, close to the forest, along with the new growth of tall grass, geometrical outlines emerged from the ground: smaller and larger square shapes and others that were completed on one side with a semicircle. Viewed from the house, these outlines, gently swaying in the breeze, appeared to hover above the ground among the pale green tips of the new forest grass. The idea of an overgrown, abandoned graveyard (like one we had passed in a neighbouring village), now only preserved in the sketchwork of the vegetation, was reinforced when we walked among the outlines in the grass. In places, beneath the soles of our feet, we thought we could trace the firmer edges of graves in the soft forest floor. Even when I started in with a spade and began to uncover an edging of old Brandenburg bricks, I was still reluctant to accept what could hardly now be denied. My archaeological research had brought to light not graves, but pre-war flower beds. I consoled myself with the thought that T. S. Eliot must have already sensed the remarkable similarities between flower beds and graves when, in *The Waste Land*, he asks if the corpse that had been buried the previous year has begun to bud: 'Will it bloom this year?' However, despite resolving the mystery, something of the idea remained floating over the outlines preserved in the grasses. Since then, at any rate, this back third of the garden has been for me the kind of place Eliot might have had in mind in 'The Burial of the Dead'. As some people visit cemeteries to reflect, to stop a moment, to connect with the past, or simply go in search of peace and quiet, whenever I feel so inclined, I walk among these outlines. Sometimes I squat down in one of the softly overgrown squares and look up into the ancient crowns of the pine forest. It is as if I, myself, had sprouted in that place and possessed some deep connection to the earth like the grass which, while I crouch down, comes up to my ears. No one sees me; the clearing is closed off on all sides.

6.

The clearing is a space: of creatures, of noises, of deceleration, a dwelling place in the open air. Sounds come from the two railway lines that run nearby. At night, you hear the clanking of freight wagons and the thump-thump of the rails on their sleepers. In the morning, the birds' terrorising in the trees. From where we sleep, under the roof tiles, we can hear the beating of pigeons' wings. In the morning, as the dew rises, voices come from the moraines: skinny guys playing football with their dogs' chewed-up rubber balls. At 10 a.m. an out-of-work neighbour starts cutting timber: the muffled thumping of his axe reaches beneath the house. Then noises from the tennis court a few hundred metres away, beyond a stretch of woods: the serves, the brief calls, the pleasant plopping of the rallies. At any time of day: the singsong of a circular saw, rhythmic, quick; firewood being trimmed to stove length. Apart from keeping dogs, this is the favourite pastime of people living round here. As well as their gas or oil heating, there is hardly anyone who does not still have their old stove, for economic reasons partly, but more than that: who knows what the future holds? Also familiar is a prolonged, steady thrumming until one of the small, single-engine aircraft appears over the treetops, on clear days towing gliders into the air from the nearby airfield. From the 'gliders hill', near Saarmund, a bald-headed terminal moraine, the brave can achieve lift-off in the oldest fashion, hurling themselves down the incline. In the 1980s, when one of these would-be Otto Lilienthals had managed to reach West Berlin, twenty kilometres away, the moraine hill was swiftly cordoned off.

7.

At the end of spring, when the forest grasses begin to mature and they bow and blend into waves that begin to brown in the sunshine, the outlines of my grave beds disappear. They were laid out in the very early days: 'Villa Hoeft' and '1923', the year the house was constructed, are inscribed on a small marble plaque to the left of the front door. In 1984, Arendt died in one of the smaller upstairs rooms, which had been a children's room, then it was a study, then a death room and now it is being used as a children's room again. After Arendt's death, during the renovation of the house, the crumbling 'Schönbrunn Palace' yellow of the facade, which at the rear of the house was overgrown with ivy, was removed and the original marble plaque was hidden beneath the new render. Not much is known about Dr Bernhard Hoeft, whose year of death is recorded as 1945 though even the circumstances of his dying remain unclear. He was an academic in Berlin and wrote novels with such titles as *There Went a Sower* and *Father and Son*. In retirement, he devoted himself entirely to his passion, namely Leopold von Ranke. Hoeft's estate, now kept in the Prussian Privy State Archives, consists of a number of boxes filled with thousands of handwritten pages, all of them Hoeft's copying out of minutes of meetings, doctoral vivas and correspondence featuring Ranke: 'Concerning the Magna Carta, the Cd. likewise supplied good answers; less satisfactory were his replies on the English Revolution . . .' – for a moment on 25 February 1847 it seemed the candidate, Theodor Neumann from Görlitz, might not pass, but Ranke and the faculty extended their mercy. One of the boxes contains copies of letters variously to Mrs Klara Ranke, to the publishing house Hoffmann und Campe and even to King Friedrich Wilhelm IV, to whom Ranke, 'in deepest devotion', presented the third volume of his *History of France*. Apart from a few tiny exclamation marks in the margins and an inscrutable system of pencil crosses, Hoeft himself remains invisible in these pages. His handwriting is controlled, compact, orderly. However, the excessive copying of all this material with the least connection to Ranke's affairs was not without its impact on Dr Hoeft's own writing style. The last of his books, on *Ranke's Appointment to Munich*, begins with a graceful: 'It was not, really, in the least surprising that . . .' This was published in 1940. In 1945, the Red Army rolls into Wilhelmshorst with a couple of tanks, one from each direction. The Willmann dairy is hit and has to be demolished. The victorious forces establish an ammunition depot on the central Goetheplatz. What would become known as the Huchel House, the comparatively remote 'Villa Hoeft', becomes the officers' HQ. All trace of Hoeft himself disappears at this point. Even his daughter cannot provide information as to her father's whereabouts; her mother never spoke of it, nor about why, very soon after, the house was auctioned off to become the property of the local savings bank. After the occupying forces move in, the daughter, then a fifteen-year-old girl, spends several days beneath the rabbit hutch of a neighbouring house. The Russian commander known as Curly Johnny, or 'Syphilis for All', is roaming the pine woods beyond the house and on the lookout for women in hiding.

8.

Rain soothes the forest, and the forest soothes the house. The dampened woods grow softer, heavier. The rain stirs a growing murmur in the vaulting pines, a sound that envelops us while, up above, the breeze passes. Every year the dampness pushes a few exotic growths up through the moss and the rippling forest grass: the grave beds open up. Tufts of seeded alyssum, blue poppies and two rhubarb stems spring up – the old, overgrown beds make a show of what they still harbour. Snails congregate on the rhubarb stems and around strawberry plants. The strawberries are vestiges of a later, smaller-scale cultivation from the time of the poet Arendt, something his young wife is said to have established in the year before his death. I had once before noticed how snails are associated with graves in a cemetery in the west of Ireland, at the foot of Mount Brandon. In the pouring rain, we visited a coastal graveyard behind the village of Fahamore. As with every plot of ground there, the cemetery is enclosed by a stone wall, beyond which, in this case, the rolling surf began immediately. There were recent graves and older, dilapidated tombs, caved in, revealing a glimpse of bones. The rain eased off, but a stiff wind blew up, so the children had to cling on to the tall, narrow grave-stones. As I was wandering around, I spotted a few black snails in the grass, a rare cluster, or so I thought. Then I looked more closely and saw the grass was overrun with processions of snails crawling out of the gaping tombs. Evidently, the weather suited them, or perhaps it gave them an opportunity to wash, to mate, to get some fresh air, or simply to relocate from an older to a more recent grave. Then gulls began to circle over the cemetery and we headed off.

Even sheltered beneath the vault of the pines, the snails are at the mercy of the birds. There are birds that move with such speed between the trees you wonder how they manage not to collide with them. Their shadowy flight seems to set the foliage in motion. Suddenly they appear in the clearing: first, a soft, almost inaudible rustling of flight, then the shadow of a small, fist-sized body in the air, and, before you actually glimpse them, they have already vanished into the far side of the wood. In the garden, if no one disturbs them, they use the brick surface of the terrace to break open the snails' shells. They hurl them from their beaks onto the bricks until they shatter or gape wide enough for them to extract the soft body from its socket. Flies and ants mop up the sticky remains. When we sit outside in the evening, the shards of snail shells crunch under our feet.

Before the war, people would sit to the side of the house, beneath a huge pine tree. A bench and a table, large enough for meals, are said to have stood there. But since that time, the forest has washed over the spot and advanced right up to the house. Hardly any of the old trees remain unscathed: galvanised hooks, a pulley with a porcelain insert for a washing line, a white scar in the beech bark where it will not close over a nail. In amongst it all can be found the scribbling of insects, the thin, clear lines on the inside of fragments of bark that we read the moment they drop from dead trees into the undergrowth, where they add to the land register of this forest plot.

9.

Perhaps Hoeft, the Ranke researcher, also provided drawings for the layout of his house. If so, it is 'not, really, in the least surprising' that the interior and exterior, as well as the individual rooms, do not properly fit together. More confusion arises as a result of the various partition walls installed after the time of the officers' HQ which created additional rooms for the accommodation of relocated people. Each room is misshapen, full of corners and alcoves. A load-bearing wall runs towards a window, swerves at the last moment and an alcove emerges in which the radio had its place in Huchel's time. In front of it, there are two armchairs and a small table, the top of which is made of ceramic tiles. Here, on the upper floor, beside the radio, Huchel would gather with his guests for cognac and coffee after dinner. It was a sort of smoking room, although smoking was pursued throughout the house, regardless of location. Cigarettes always had to be available and, if they ran out, one of the children would take the train through the woods to Wannsee to buy a new pack of Gold Dollar. The photographer Roger Melis's images have recorded and preserved the radio's position and some of the guests too: Huchel with Böll, Huchel with Frisch, Huchel with Kundera, etc. Huchel later suspected that there were 'bugs' in the ceiling and in the telephone. To make surveillance more difficult, the radio was turned on during conversations.

'Today I remember the dead in my house'. So begins a marvellous elegy by Octavio Paz that speaks of the dead, but also of time running out:

> Between door and death there's little space
> and hardly time enough to sit,
> to lift your head, to look at the clock
> and to discover: a quarter past eight.

Bearing witness to things handed down from the past, and to the house itself, is an ambivalent business. Which of us wants to be continually reminded of the past, or to be made so aware that the time we are given will vanish in a moment: 'a quarter past eight'? Perhaps, as a glance at the history of the genre suggests, it is the kind of people who engage in the writing of poetry. In a house that has itself become a kind of ancestral shrine to literature, you find yourself talking to the dead whose work is already integral to any such conversation. This leads to a strange sort of interference. Paz's poem states:

> Your silence is the mirror of my life,
> in my life your dying persists:
> I am the last error in your erring.

The 'last error'? Should there be some sort of comfort to be found in that? Perhaps, in the end, you might prefer to 'pass away' in the proper sense of the phrase and be the 'last'. Then, suddenly, it is 'a quarter past eight' and the door has closed. And the party goes on noisily in some other room.

10.

'Why, Antaeus, this place, all day long / speaking through the forks of branches?' begins a poem I started, and later abandoned, about living under the pine vault. Since the renovation work on the house, the roof has been broken up by a row of windows. Under them stands the desk; you sit there, in the topmost third of the forest.

The movement of the treetops before your eyes is dizzying and the house starts to sway. During storms, the timber joints crack ominously, and you say to yourself: the roof-tree is buckling. When it rains, we sit here as if under canvas, in a place of shelter, yet everything is enveloped in the noise of the downpour. In among the oaks that face the road, the rain falls more noisily than in the pines – the pines hold steady beneath the downpour. In summer, when the weather is better, the quality of light in the branches shifts endlessly. Light falls through budding leaves in a palimpsest that towers over us and around us, slowly shifting with the sun through the course of the day. In the evening, the lit-up flanks of the trees show a dark yellow colour, of the kind you might find in a painting by Bonnard. Later still, the tops of the pines redden and, in the last moments (so briefly you are not sure if you imagined it), they glow blood-red, then are dark to their very tips.

Huchel wrote in a room under this same roof. At midday, the poet would come down the 'decrepit stairs', as he says in the poem 'Hubertusweg', and mutter lines to himself at the table, lines his wife immediately wrote down and then turned into typescript. With this draft, the master disappeared back up to his room for the afternoon. With more completed drafts, he would continue on down to the editorial office, located on the ground floor. There he would dictate the text to his secretary, Frau Narr, who, as Huchel's editorial colleague from Potsdam Fritz Erpel reports, even insisted on using the Duden dictionary's spelling for poems. When Huchel worked in the editorial office on *Sinn und Form*, he would jot down lines of poetry or individual words on scraps of paper. When visitors arrived, these scraps – that had over time become scattered here and there – had to be gathered up for safekeeping. In the post-war period, Huchel was upset when he discovered lines and images from his poems had been plagiarised in a book by Karl Krolow. The theft came from poems that had already been published, at the start of the 1930s, in *Die literarische Welt* and the magazine *Die Kolonne*. Since that period, Huchel had been known as a poet, even though his first collection – called simply *Poems*

(*Gedichte*) – did not make an appearance until 1948, when he was already forty-six years old.

Opposite the writing room is the so-called 'eye', a small window, arched over by a gentle curve of the roof and hence slightly rounded at the top; through it, you look down onto the front of the property. Quite hidden, you can see who is passing, who stops, or who is at the gate. When I climb the steep, 'decrepit' stairs up to the attic, there is a stone that can be seen through the eye window – though only from a particular spot, on the last but one step – an erratic that Huchel had picked out on a walk as his gravestone and brought back into the garden. Then the view framed by the tiny window reminds me of Robert Frost's poem 'Home Burial': 'The little graveyard where my people are! / So small the window frames the whole of it. / Not so much larger than a bedroom, is it?' Anyone who reads Frost's 'pastoral', along with Joseph Brodsky's commentary on it, will learn just about everything there is to know about movement, dramatic impact and the handling of perspective within a poem. And although there are frequent references to the characteristically American in Frost's poetry, his book, *North of Boston*, does not seem to me to be far removed from this locality.

To the right of the erratic, on the right-hand edge of the picture framed by the eye, lies the manhole cover over the water meter; to the left is the gate and the driveway. In the middle of the picture, at the front of the house, stands the column of a single pine tree like the big hand of a clock, at an angle, a little after the hour. At midday and then again in the evening, bells automatically ring out from the little church on the Goetheplatz, built during the Nazi era. At the ringing of the bells, the dogs also strike up. First, there is a single, short burst from across the street, or perhaps one street further over, then neighbouring dogs follow suit; finally, a great chorus envelops the village which might as well be coming from a pack of wolves. It is said the wolves are set to return to the woods in this area. They are following the exact same routes as their ancestors. But not much really happens in 'the eye'. Twice a day, sometimes as early as eight o'clock in the morning, a dog-owning couple pass, walking their two white poodles. Then, at noon, the post arrives. In the evening, the lights come on along the street, the twilight shift.

11.

Once, perhaps, there really was something about this place that lay beyond time and its events, in other words – 'outside'. 'Out in the woods of Wilhelmshorst, never travelling and seemingly immoveable,' writes Hans Mayer of Huchel, he was still 'a decade ahead of his far busier literary contemporaries.' The apparent contradiction between being 'ahead' and being 'on the outside' brings to mind a marvellous observation made by Hermann Lenz: 'Whoever stands still, leaps far ahead in time.' While Mayer's remark recalls the timeline we used to have at school, with its implied obligation to make progress, in Lenz's comment you can also see the possibility of taking your time, while standing still, time to consider your own direction of travel. 'The transformations of the self are the essence of time,' wrote Günter Eich in his *Remarks on Poetry* (*Bemerkungen uber Lyrik*) in 1932, and he went on: 'The transformations of the self are the business of the lyric poet.' Even if later Eich did not foreground such ideas, they nevertheless appear, towards the end of the 1950s, as the basis of what he calls 'the anarchist's instinctive feeling of resentment'. Eich, too, had tried to settle 'outside'. Of course, this 'outside' had nothing to do with 'escaping the world', nothing to do with an idyll beyond the metropolitan. The poet friends Huchel, Eich and Martin Raschke had distanced themselves from the late Expressionist mainstream and the New Objectivity and also from the presumed association of modernity

23

with the city. But not out of any traditionalism. Eich was a tech-nophile and had a passion for cars; Huchel and Eich were among the first to make use of the new medium of radio for their work. Conscious of the formal possibilities, they were concerned with a modernity without the obvious trappings of modernism used by other new poets who wanted to prove themselves as being 'on the cutting edge'.

Thoughts of being 'outside' run through Huchel's statements and his correspondence. 'As you know, Ingeborg Bachmann and Enzensberger were on the outside along with me,' he wrote in a letter in March 1959. Huchel was particularly impressed by Bachmann ('Have you noticed, a forehead like Trakl's, that exhaus-tion, whiteness . . .'), though she immediately had to return to Berlin for forgotten luggage before they could travel together to Leipzig, to visit Hans Mayer as planned. A letter to Rudolf Leonhard shows how differently this sense of being 'outside' might be viewed: 'My request that you visit me out here, in the midst of my many children and cats, is, as ever, made in vain, though as ever, I must add: only 28 minutes from Wannsee!' Leonhard: '28 minutes from Wannsee, but how many trains a day? And then how much further to walk? And getting to Wannsee is nothing? It's a day trip . . .' When the telephone was out of order – for whatever reason – communication with the city appeared to break down completely: 'Today I learned from the fault service that *my ability to speak to Berlin* will not be restored for several days.' Hanns Eisler replies: 'Your inaccessibility in Michendorf does nothing to lighten my spirits either.' Arnold Zweig's letter from 1963 goes even further. It is one of the few dec-larations of solidarity sent to Huchel after his forced resignation as editor-in-chief, though Zweig opens with the words: 'As you well know, on many occasions, I was critical of the fact that our *Sind und Form* was based *in a remote corner, out beyond Michendorf*.' Since Michendorf was already an almost Bohemian village from the point of view of Berlin, the precision of 'beyond Michendorf', indeed 'in a remote corner', lends it the sense of belonging to some Nirvana in the minds of the capital's literati. After the Wall had been built, after Huchel's political stigmatisation and resulting isolation, Wilhelmshorst really did become a place of 'Exile': 'Come evening, friends close in, / the shadows of hills. / Slowly they press across the threshold, / darkening the salt, darkening the bread / and with my silence they strike up a conversation.'

Nowadays, in truth, 'on the outside' only signifies on the outskirts, a part of the greater Berlin metropolitan area. Along the old road – once a designated corridor for West Germans to reach West Berlin, now three lanes wide in each direction – we cover the forty kilometres to Berlin-Mitte in forty-five minutes. At the Mittelgraben, beyond Langerwisch, banks of fog drift across the road as we near the motorway. It is not uncommon here to see bunches of flowers beneath the trees, vases half-spilled, a valedictory note in a transparent plastic envelope splattered with dirt. On the outskirts: there is now a restlessness that seems to underlie the heaped moraines, a murmuring, a muttering to the tips of the nettles, to the heads of surveyors, to their poles. Everywhere you look, something is disappearing: tags attached to tree trunks indicate those soon to be felled. Infill development, the expansion of urban boundaries, the tendering of proposals for new-build sites. Come evening, the green- and red-lit aircraft high overhead, apparently motionless, look like Christmas trees in the air as they stack in holding patterns above the city.

In his own, more profound sense, Peter Huchel has remained 'on the outside' to this day, eluding our grasp. To this day, he remains averted: present in the house, but more usually in some other room. I do not remember a single remark in all the accounts of those who were his friends that would suggest they had really 'got close' to him. We know little of his private life; hardly any details of it feature in his letters. Despite his intense work with the many contributors to *Sinn und Form*, inevitably not without conflict in the course of daily business, Huchel kept his life 'on the outside in Wilhelmshorst' firmly under wraps. This is despite the fact that he was always an amusing and engaging storyteller in his dealings with the staff in his editorial office, or indeed with the village people he encountered on his walks across the fields – at least, that is how he is remembered.

12.

'October, November, / the lungs of autumn / breathe out fog.' In the clearing behind the house, where it lingers among the pine trees, we breathe the fog which, like the pine trees and their damp, are such frequent elements in Huchel's poetry. In late autumn, before the first snow falls, I rake the leaves from the back third of the garden, close to the forest. I want to make sure that, come spring, the forest grasses will be able to grow up into the breeze undisturbed, above the outlines of the grave beds. So that their outlines are not interfered with, I collect fallen branches and sweep decaying leaves into a corner of the garden. To aerate the soil, I use a pointed iron stick to prick and poke holes into the moss that suffocates the sandy soil here, stifling the grass and everything underneath. Then, once I have started, and as if of its own volition, the raking continues – beyond the flower beds, across the lawn to the terrace and onto the paths leading to the front garden of the house, the state of which is important in forming people's opinions, I mean, determining our reputation in the village and, believe it or not, the reputation of the poet whose name this house still bears. My overgrown, in fact invisible flower beds and the taking care of their sporadic, spontaneous legacies have made a gardener of me.

'Where you stand, dig deep!' advises Friedrich Nietzsche, because there one can be quite 'undaunted'. On 6 January 2000, at Epiphany, the day of the Three Magi, I planted our Christmas tree – which we had purchased complete with its rootstock and had dragged laboriously up the steps into the house. I planted it at the back of my grave beds. My own first planting which, in the layering process of time, now marks the beginning of a new millennium. The work was as hard as counting down to the millennium. It was like starting a long-term project from scratch. First, the digging of a hole for the roots, large enough to be able to line it with a layer of good dark topsoil. Then, scattering fertiliser into the hole, the skin and ground-up hooves, nails and horns of dead animals, all by-products from the abattoir and purchased on the advice of the garden centre, shrink-wrapped in a two-kilo bag at the same time as I bought our millennium tree. The following spring, I planted a second tree, which now stands halfway between the grave beds and the vegetable beds which were laid out nearer the house during the Huchel era.

On the floor of the clearing, on the terrace, on the walls and the floorboards of the house, even on our faces, the forest's shadow theatre plays its shifting patterns, its silent film, which the sun projects through the vault of pine needles and branches. At first, you think: how could anyone ever learn to read under these boughs, in this clearing with its flower beds, stunted fruit trees and old vegetable plants, hunkered down in the grassy soil, within the hunter's hide of history and of silence, at one with the swinging of the pendulum at its turning point. Yet, as Francis Ponge writes about the pine forest: 'Everything here, without exaggeration, is created so you surrender yourself . . . Nothing anecdotal. Everything here curbs curiosity, yet at the same time without wilfulness, and that *in the midst of nature*, without clear division, without deliberate isolation, without grand gesture, without inhibition.'

So, you stand back, you yield, you begin to disentangle yourself from proceedings. In the nerve bundles of three trees: outlines of lives, raw recordings of an unfamiliar territory, the place from which my writing speaks.

(2003)

HUCHEL AND THE DUMMY BRIDGE

Perhaps genuine reading experiences are so rare because they are based not only on what is read, but also on what is lived. Some people may never have experienced anything of the kind and that is precisely why they, all the more diligently, go on making literature. Their gaze flickers across the printed texts of the greats of art, science and philosophy, and a new text eventually emerges on which they inscribe their own name. Yet the reader of such readers will become aware of this at some stage and then cry out, as in Franz Kafka's story of 'The Unmasking of a Conman': 'I know you!' But how do we know it? 'And my companion acquiesced to this on his own behalf and – with a smile – on my behalf too, reaching his right arm up along the wall, leaning his cheek close beside it, closing his eyes. But I did not wait for the end of that smile, suddenly shame caught me up. It was only because of the smile that I knew he was nothing but a conman.' Perhaps it is this posturing, all amicable insistence, above all the desire for art as he leans against the bookshelves, closes his eyes and smiles – 'I know you!'

When I first began to be interested in literature, I purchased books indiscriminately from the LEUNA Works lending library for one mark per item, books which had been withdrawn from stock, including Peter Huchel's *Poems* (*Gedichte*), published by Aufbau in 1948. That book, already a rarity at the time, had two stamps inside it: 'Checked against the list of prohibited literature, April 1, 1946' and 'Withdrawn 1983'. In between these two dates, there were just three loans recorded. I, as the fourth, was to be allowed to carry it off with me to the autumn camp of our so-called Pioneer Building Battalion – this was the reason I was purchasing the books. I was the driver of a five-tonne W50 Ballon truck, loaded with sections of a remarkable and, in the East, it was said, quite unique fake bridge. The Huchel was stuffed under the felt of the engine housing that separated the driver's seat from the passenger seat. The book still smells of the diesel which, during pre-ignition, we had to pump in by the litre to get the engine started from cold. In the frequent stops on our way to the camp beside the river, where we were to construct our precious bridge, piece by piece (and, it was rumoured, this had never yet been done successfully), I began to read. Never since those eighteen months I was compelled to spend in barracks have I known a reading experience so disconnected from the passage of time. A reading experience almost outside time: the stops lasted for hours when one of the trucks broke down: 'I saw the glory of war / as the basket-hilt of Death's sabre' – I read and I grew conscious of the weight of our strange caravan as it crawled forwards. Huchel's post-war images of the treks of the defeated and the displaced, the bones of the dead beside desolate roads, troubled the threadbare blanket we laid over our fears at night, a covering rent by each attack drill in those first terrifying moments of what seemed to be the 'real thing'.

When we had reached the river, the attempt to construct the dummy bridge, which none of us had any experience of, started immediately and it absorbed all three weeks of our time in camp. All this, of course, was carried out under 'combat conditions', which meant that I, as a driver, was basically not allowed to leave my truck. So, after unloading, I turned it round and for three weeks stared down through the November fogs towards the river, to where my comrades were struggling with the components of the bridge. To escape feeling brain-dead before this yawning expanse of nothingness, coffee liqueur was passed around and I either sank back into a kind of rigor mortis or I read and muttered Huchel to myself:

> Mute, accusing, leaves of trees.
> Freezing, lonely, moss-thick ground.
> High above the hunters' ways,
> hunting now, a stranger hound.
>
> Everywhere on dampened sand,
> lie the forest's powder burns,
> bullet-like, the scattered acorns.
>
> Autumn softly fired its rounds,
> shots above the burial place.
>
> Hark, the dead, their rustling crowns,
> fogs and demons drifting close.

In the process, sitting in my truck, the window through which I gazed down on the bridge was transformed into a kind of TV screen in which the whole scene gradually took on the qualities of a fiction, including nature. What I saw were dummy trees, the dummy river with its dummy bank opposite and dummy soldiers who were supposed to bridge it with their dummy bridge. Unlike Huchel, who was drawn to the mysticism of Jakob Böhme and the belief that, in humans and animals and plants, outward appearances correspond to an inner form, I saw nothing but dummy figures engaged in a bewildering performance. Huchel sought to translate the landscape – and with it the essence of things – into language, into outer form. After two weeks, grown delirious with vast amounts of coffee liqueur and nothingness, I embarked on an attempt to construct my own counterbalance, an autonomous interpretation of things, and I wrote my first poem. I remember it was supposed to be about the fact that we, in our facile way, too quickly furnish things with a meaning, so that their reality grows ever more obscured, etc. I was able to begin with our legendary bridge because it *was* a dummy. We were good at dummies in general: for weeks now, we had dug the ground and heaped up tanks and anti-aircraft gun emplacements. In the winter months, we had to pour water over our dirt-pile tanks, equipped as they were with pine-trunk cannons and anti-aircraft guns, so that they would *set firm*. Dummies were our speciality. Dummies had featured as the main constituent in our basic training before we spent the remainder of our 'honorary service' year shovelling carbide in the BUNA and LEUNA chemical plants. In the enemy's aerial viewfinders appeared whole units of heavy artillery which we had *conjured from the ground*.

After two weeks at our riverside camp, the landscape around me had taken on a wholly fictional character. Over and over, I read Huchel, 'ceaseless shadows, roaming through / crags and rivers . . ', and I realised that his poems already had a countersense written into them. A procession of shadowy figures, with leaves and ashes round their feet, marched through the text of 'Havel Night' so that, in the sound of each step, its diminishing significance became audible, taking us back to childhood, to prehistory, back to the dead: 'near the ghost that roars by night / diving still into its river'.

'By the Saale's bright shore . . ', the demonic and ghostly nature of 'Havel Night', as Huchel has it roar through his poem, now also lay upon our river, something Joseph von Eichendorff might perhaps have approved of, though not so much situated there in an obscure valley beyond Dessau, but rather viewed from above, in daylight, from one of the rocky paths around Giebichenstein.

'Scent from distant, by-gone ages / stooping here into the waters. / Stepping down, we move in silence, / evening's liquor sweeping through us.' Late one evening, at the end of our third week, thoroughly swept through with the endless waiting, with the drinking and the reading, I watched as our journeymen's piece, our most precious dummy, was slowly pushed out onto the river: it lasted all of ten seconds before it broke up under the pressure of the current. A few floating drums with their couplings and bolt-on grilles had been supposed to suggest – from high in the air – an armoured pontoon bridge, a bridge that was merely the image of a bridge and of significance only on the 10 x 10 centimetre screens in the cockpits of Tornadoes.

Experts have claimed that such dummies were used very successfully by the Serbians during the Bosnian War. When – at the height of the air raids on the Balkans – Martin Walker of *The Guardian* wanted to know, at a press conference, why NATO was deploying its million-dollar weaponry to combat artillery constructed from telegraph poles and cartwheels, I thought of Huchel and his poems.

(1999)

'THE POST-WAR ERA NEVER ENDS':
ON JÜRGEN BECKER

1. AHRENSHOOP AND HAMBURG

It was in Ahrenshoop on the Baltic Sea, in June 1997, that I first met Jürgen Becker. After our poetry reading, we stood outside the art gallery and smoked. We talked about American literature, about Donald Barthelme and about an 'international poetry festival' in New York, and how the poet Nicolas Born, it is said, adapted that description to the more apt 'international drinking festival'. We talked about the summer, the weather, our travel plans. I said: 'Ireland, Dingletown . . .' I think Jürgen Becker replied something like: 'You can't go everywhere.' Then we drove to the neighbouring village for dinner; we had wild boar from the nearby Darss Forest and Lübzer Pils. I told him I had once seen the wild boar swimming across to Hiddensee with their snouts sticking up out of the water. Though a mention of unfamiliar places, at least places never visited, can sometimes lead to a lull in the conversation, my story had the opposite effect. *Rügen, Hiddensee*: where did you stay, what did you see, what has changed, yet it's still as it was, etc.

We drove out along the old *Panzerplatten* roads (where concrete slabs had been laid on dirt roads to carry the weight of tanks) through the hinterland of the Darss, not far from the Bodden shore. When I read Jürgen Becker's poems these days, I think he would have liked to note down a word like *Panzerplatten* (just as references to the *scissors telescope* or to *plane-table maps* are recurring favourites in his poems). I also think he would have been interested to know that roads built with the same conically shaped slabs were common in East Germany as routes linking the more remote villages. Knowing Jürgen Becker's poems, as I do today, I think he would have enjoyed discussing the landscape, noting similarities to the countryside near Prora, near Greifswald, around Stralsund: 'the beginnings of a journey into the landscape'. We might have stopped and got out of the car to take a closer look at the markings on the slabs and read in them something about their provenance, the strength of the concrete, seeing their rain-filled hollows with the iron loops at the bottom for the construction cranes' hooks and the Baltic Sea sky reflected in the surface of the water: 'Huge, then shrinking geography'.

But I am already speaking from my experience of reading Becker; I am moving too fast, and before I go on to consider the fundamental elements of a Jürgen Becker poem, I will rewind a few years and explain how it was I first encountered his work. In Berlin, in the summer of 1990, on the eve of German monetary union, I was a guest of the poet Elke Erb. We got into a discussion about what the new circumstances might mean for a writer who had grown up in the East. To be more precise, the question arose of what it was we ought to be catching up on. Above the kitchen table where we were sitting, there were two drawings: jungle scenes, elephants with riders. Elke Erb said: 'What you need to become familiar with are Jung's dream interpretation and Jürgen Becker's poems.' The next day, on the first day of monetary union, I drove to Hamburg, where we had both been invited to an East–West German Studies student conference in which, on this occasion, 'young people' would also be taking an active part. I remember the awkwardness of the situation that morning, arriving in Hamburg without any valid currency. The last of my 'welcome money' – 100 Deutschmarks, which after the border had been opened every East German citizen had been able to collect on the presentation of his or her identity card – had been spent long ago. To make matters worse, I had left details of the conference location (as well as all the 'conference materials') back in Berlin. In my diary, I found the telephone number of a West German colleague who, I had been informed, would be 'responsible for any questions or problems we had'. When we parted, I had once more got hold of some 'foreign currency', in a sense my second 'welcome money', on the occasion of my first actual trip across the former inner-German border. Among the other things I bought, and this takes us back to the subject of Jürgen Becker, was my first Becker collection with the strangely apt title, *Poem of the Reunified Landscape* (*Das Gedicht von der wiedervereinigten Landschaft*).

I remember being baffled by the loose form of this long poem divided into five sections. I liked long poems – that was not the problem – it was the internal structure, the construction of it. I thought: 'Isn't this too incoherent, too loosely put together?' The tone of voice: so casual, a lot of it sounding spoken, lifted from conversations, from everyday speech, from the commonplace world of thought and its reiterated expressions. As I have said, I was encountering the poem without preconceptions, I mean, without any knowledge of previous Becker texts, neither his statement of poetic principles as it had been made about forty years before,[1] nor his early books which implemented those poetics. So I was reading my way into the poem, quite unprepared, and from then right through to today, shall we say, I have slowly been asking myself questions and coming to understand a few things.

> . . . every day
> the new impressions; a long-term poem that

has tapped into all the correspondences . . . ? The approach,
which is this talking to myself, scattered
across diary pages, taking down quotes and rough maps
as on a beer mat; fragments of an evening
on the phone, occasions for postcards and
a few letters . . .
              the hushed talk
in touch with the Heinkel pilots . . .

Between our sessions at the conference and the World Cup's closing matches (as if there wasn't enough happening all at once), I began to realise why it was Elke Erb who had pointed me towards Becker. It was connected to something I had understood from Erb's own phrase about 'a life-text'. In its methods, Becker's style of writing was not unlike Erb's 'procedural' texts: this long poem was a process that integrated both immediate and more distant modalities of language, his own voice along with materials drawn from other sources such as events, photos, maps (ever present), as well as interjections from neighbouring rooms, from the mail, the news, weather conditions and whatever else strayed within range of his poetic imagination. In all, an attempt to bring a 'natural' disposition into his poem. The openness of the form allows the text to stage itself, as it were, to proceed accompanied by the observation of its own gestures and concerns. As its movements unfolded, perceptual developments, theoretical thinking and more reflective passages were all synthesised. Becker staged a tableau in which that 'whereof one must be silent' was being ushered towards the point of articulation. And often the point of departure for the poem was speech as a process, as a proclamation in its proper sense. The one who spoke to himself did so, in the first place, simply to continue being present; a grasping for the most immediate, simplest affirmation with which a text might begin and then proceed. The voice takes on an inductive role: something is first uttered, then we listen in for more, a 'speech that is in search of words that are already present' (Becker). If, at this point, the 'relaxed field' between the powers of intuition and of conscious recall arises, then the poem can begin:

> or everything goes wrong
> in the scheme of things, which has failed to organise the
>   absent fields
> of your experience. What is missing, if we
> are talking about it, is lying somewhere forgotten; perhaps
> the light of the crescent moon was so feeble then that I
> did not see the tears on a face beyond the window;
> perhaps you were not aware of your journey
> suddenly coming to an end, because earlier and much closer
> than usual the tawny owl revealed itself in the midst
> of the pear tree. Certainly, the walk through the cemetery
>   was fine,
> but what had to be done was not a search for something
> we had missed; we revealed carved letters, cleared stones
> and tidied the hedge . . .

For Becker, it is not the reconstruction of the past or what's given that is at issue, but the endlessly 'missing remainder', the ability to allow things to approach, however and wherever they present themselves. In such a process, narrative is preserved but as a gesture, often without authority, in the shifting interchange of perspectives. This is precisely what the loosened syntax with its light-as-a-feather linkages allows, a continuous enabling of departures, circlings-back and changes of direction. But in the openness and lightness of Becker's poems I had, as I said, at first seen an excessive levity. It was my view at the time that writing was more a matter of steeling oneself, of making one's text 'watertight', sealing it off against possible exterior influences. To achieve this, one might resort to traditional forms and it was because of this that formalism was important to me. I suppose the whole thing sprang ultimately from an ingrained self-limitation, a rather dispiriting aversion to the realities that surrounded us as we wrote, something that I fell into in the mid-eighties. As an example of this kind of approach (and it is easy to laugh at this from today's perspective), the precious, dark blue, pre-war edition of Stefan George's work had pride of place on the shelf in my student room in Halle. Becker's declaration of poetic principles in 1963 sought to reject obligations to the art form altogether. There is no doubt that this approach could only have arisen from an essentially different context: an open and, indeed, progressively more open society, one to whose pluralistic spirit one might contribute artistically in what Sibylle Cramer, in a discussion of Becker's work, has called the 'democratic norm of art'. The question has yet to be settled whether and to what degree styles of writing – which, in any case, vary so greatly from author to author – are determined by differing social contexts; but what is certain is that the underlying preconditions of my own and of Becker's writing, up to this point, were utterly different.

Also, perhaps, there could have been no more disorienting context for my first reading of Jürgen Becker than that Hamburg conference. I was announced on the programme as due to deliver a paper on structuralism, which seemed to be a subject of interest to my colleagues in the West. But, at short notice, I decided to switch my topic and spoke instead on the literature of the younger generation in the East. The West German professors did not know much about it; perhaps it was not as interesting to them as structuralism. On the other hand, the East German professors did not know who Botho Strauss was, although *The Young Man*, for example, had been published by the East German publishers Aufbau Verlag.

Even so, we were given a very friendly welcome in Hamburg. It is clearer to me now than it was at the time that what predominated on both sides was curiosity. One wondered what kind of people the other Germans were and that was, ultimately, much more interesting than structuralism. West Germany won the World Cup and Hamburg remained my one and only academic conference, no doubt partly because of the *Poem of the Reunified Landscape*.

2. SPATIAL THINKING AND MY FORMER SELF

Besides the confusions and difficulties that are part of this story of reading Becker's poetry, there were also things that immediately drew me to it. First of all, its reading of place: Ostend, Oderbruch, Paulinzella, Erfurt, Jüterbog, Wiepersdorf, Niederer Fläming, Berlin, the Belgian coast, Zella-Mehlis, Putbus, etc. Becker's technique is to 'lay out' a place in the poem and to read from there the landscape's memory, in order to spatialise history 'on the ground', so that the remembrance inherent in the landscape and the reminiscences of the observer interrogate each other and are brought to speech.

Within this space, the conventional chronology is suspended and the remembered and the visible rub up against each other. In order to present them together, Becker dissolves the narrative to such a degree that, in a constant process of interchange, sequences from different times float loose effortlessly and reassemble. The poems, often several pages long, are structured with this in mind: they are open, permeable, casual in tone, unconstrained in their development.

Take, for example, 'Dressel's Garden', a poem from *Foxtrot in Erfurt's Stadium* (1993), set on the east side of Erfurt, with a child in a building's stairwell. There is much that is sharply delineated, but also a great deal of subtle intercutting between scenes. 'But where then?' or 'Only, how to go on?': these are the kinds of rhetorical breaks typical of Becker when he wants to effect a switch in direction or feed in new imagery in a transition to different times and places: 'Open / stands a front door and sunlight lies / on the tiles, the steps climb into the shadows / of the hallway . . .' You can walk into these poems. They open up a space and they conduct you to places where something is told, or where, you could say, you tell yourself something. You are standing in the hallway of your own childhood, or beneath the stairs, and you listen to the tread of those coming home from work late in the afternoon. Cyanide, rat poison, gleams bluishly in the corners of the cellar. A few fluted jars, a handcart, a pile of *People's Watch* waiting for the next bin collection and, in the furthest reaches of the darkness, where the sloping underside of the communal staircase and the cellar floor meet, can be found hidden riches, dead birds and last season's wrinkled conkers. Then comes Mr S, our upstairs neighbour, with his laboured steps, heavy on the left as much as the right; at each landing he expels breath from between his teeth. Then Mrs D, who was always muttering to herself, and then Aranka, who we had furtively pursued as children because of gossip about her bow legs – no more than a few sordid remarks, but with a powerful appeal, nevertheless, to our erotic fantasies.

The staircase is one of those magical places of childhood that Jürgen Becker unlocks. It is one of those places that serves a 'gateway function' in storytelling, and another such example is the stove. The process of reminiscence in Becker's story of *The Missing Remainder* (1997) always begins in the presence of the stove. When the stove enters the scene, it becomes the medium for plunging further into the story. All who have grown up with such a stove heating system have had the experience of *making a fire*. They are familiar with the materials, with wood, coal, ash; they understand the nature of the fuel, the smell of carbon dioxide, the glow of the fire and the heat that strikes them in the face before the open stove door. They know the look of the blaze before the door can be closed, and the precise timing; they know what the phrase 'stove warmth' really means. By the stove, in the stairwell, beside the fence, in the yard, at the border post, in the barn, on a platform crowded with refugees – Becker's work collects such locations as these, and they constitute a personal register of vanishing moments to be recalled. Of course, anyone could write about such things today, but it would lack the affective colouring of genuine experience, the local colour of true recollection. 'Too dark / the hallway in which stands the visitor who has only ever / dreamed, in the decades before this October, of being there / again in the stairwell of his childhood.' The being-with-yourself in the dark, in the hiding place beneath the stairs and, at the same time, to be standing on the outside, among the sounds, the fragments of sentences, the footsteps, before the names on defunct doorbells, in amongst the smells – the character of this present-past resonance chamber is a template for the perception of the world in Becker's poetry.

3. 'THE POST-WAR ERA NEVER ENDS'

'Give me tobacco leaf, a filter; the post-war / era never ends. The dew, the cold of the morning, / so begins September, the September / of quotations. // You understand ... or are you / too young? If so, watch now, how / history continues by rolling itself, exactly / in the same old way.' The Second World War began on 1 September 1939. Jürgen Becker spent both the war and the post-war period, between 1939 and 1947, in Thuringia. In his books written in the 1990s, it is his memory of this period that predominates. The poems have a calm, unhurried pace, every detail unfolding into its own particular space. The material is drawn from the many journeys Becker made to revisit the landscape of his East German childhood once the border opened in 1989. By making the process of visualising the past itself the subject of his writing, Becker gives us the sense of accompanying the journey of each poem 'at eye level'. No subsequently acquired knowledge of history has inspired these poems; the experience of history is itself returned to its authentic ground in perception and recollection:

> . . . time does not stand still
> like an old model that can be considered
> at leisure. The leaves in the meadow, at night, when
> the wind blows, are driven slowly
> and listlessly on, and you forget them as quickly as
> the din of an ideology. What remains
> must be destroyed . . .

Jürgen Becker was a child of the 'white years', as people say. In other words, his birth year meant he fell between the conscription drives of the Nazi Wehrmacht and those of the West German Federal Army and East German National People's Army (NVA), which, right up to the end of the 1950s, could only be joined as a volunteer. 'Too young to be sent to the Front, they were old enough not only to be shaped by the dictatorship, but also to be inculcated into its political-military pre-socialisation,' as the historian Paul Nolte writes. The potency of images from this time, such as the Nazi 'cub' with a hunting knife and a neckerchief or the 'Young People's Film Hour', remains undiminished for Becker. Such things play an increasingly important role in the later texts in which he summons up states of childhood consciousness from his experiences of the war and post-war years:

> *By the Saale's bright shore*
> came the first picture postcards; the emplacement
> near Leuna. Xenophon in green-painted barracks,
> keeping the home place together: 'Senftleben
> at the gate, to the right, Winne Herz'; besides that, an empty theatre
> the *Central German Stadium* in which ghosts
> ran their laps and Ilse Werner's 'Foxtrot' whistled
> from speakers above the ice rink . . .

Here again, it is the specific, concrete location in which history and its ramifications are developed, the emplacement near Leuna where the first and last cohorts of the post-war era are brought together: those same green-painted barracks where we actually lived – almost forty years after the period to which the poem refers – during our own basic military service, in the so-called *Old Place*, which had previously been the Wehrmacht barracks, subsequently turned into a prison camp, then a refugee camp, finally a camp for the NVA and, after the fall of the Wall, developed as a 'business park' – since gone bankrupt. The barracks have been demolished and only the old ordnance bunker, which the Red Army once tried in vain to destroy, remains standing:

> Much happened, but not what was expected, no more than
> was feared; once the question arose whether each day
> the newspaper was writing the next instalment of the novel
> . . . and
> what the fire-watching kid gave away in his poem,
> in which *Buna* served as a rhyme for *Leuna*.

Above all, Becker's poems are concerned with the way landscape becomes itself through history, how historical turning points are revolutions for lives *and* the land, how the image of it changes, most obviously in times of war: towns and villages disappearing or surviving, or being entirely changed, borders being relocated or imposed. The memory of the landscape and the memory of the observer interrogate each other — reading of place and spatial thinking come together for a 'provisional post-war German topography' and this is what Jürgen Becker presents us with:

> Perhaps also
> the draft of a landscape begins, parts of which,
> the memories and the longings, have been there
> for ages; you cannot simply
> take them up, because the war still goes on, though
> so many children and children's children
> no longer recognise the war.

These lines from *The English Window* (1990) remind me of an evening we spent together at the Cologne Writing Centre. Joachim Sartorius and I each read our poems, but Jürgen Becker read a kind of fantasy tale that he had written specially for the occasion about an imaginary encounter, under wartime conditions, between that evening's three writers:

'Then I am reminded of nightmarish scenarios, those imagined moments when a so-called state of emergency arises . . . My colleague from Thuringia, in his NVA uniform, might then have suddenly appeared on my doorstep in the shape of the enemy. The fakery of training exercises would suddenly no longer be merely an imagined reality and a state of war would prevail in which a poem would no longer have much to offer. It might also be perfectly plausible that Joachim Sartorius would be present in the house as a refugee who, having fled from a West Berlin recently occupied by the Red Army, has perhaps made his way into the Rhineland, to

Bergisches Land, to a small farmstead that refugees still recall from the years of the Second World War. Following orders to conduct a search of this out-of-the-way house, the NVA soldier, Seiler, might have come across a desk, a few bookshelves; perhaps . . . he might have propped his Kalashnikov in the corner, pulled out a collection of Huchel poems from his rucksack, perhaps a few handwritten sheets, and perhaps the three of us would then have sat around the table, striking up a conversation about reading and writing, and thence, under the imperceptibly emerging, gentle imperative of poetry, for a passing moment, we might have put a stop to the war.'

With irony, though without undermining the seriousness of his own concerns, Becker was here telling us something about his own writing. The fact that later Becker texts, in which the war theme dominates, are grounded in his own memories and that they promote this idea of an 'imperceptibly emerging, gentle imperative of poetry' distinguishes them from the increasing number of poems written by my own generation that tackle the war theme. In Becker's work, the material is treated differently, treated *from experience*, rather than treated superficially in terms of its possibilities as subject matter, as appealing artistic raw material. In his essay 'Air War and Literature' (published in English in the volume *On the Natural History of Destruction*), W. G. Sebald rightly highlighted a problem in the literary representation of the reality of war and set a question mark over the 'dynamic Speech Actionism' with which, for example, Arno Schmidt, in his *Scenes from the Life of a Faun*, deploys all his linguistic skills to depict the spectacle of devastation in the wake of an air raid. Sebald's objection does not arise from any kind of moralising or linguistically conservative attitude; he had in mind those 'enthusiasts' who, with potentially destructive effects and in the name of the 'avant-garde', produce texts that are impressive as showcases but manage to achieve little else. Such ambition reaps only vengeance when it addresses the theme of war in particular;

the writing swiftly becomes brittle, too obvious, the reader left dissatisfied. Becker's writing insists that we remain situated within history even as it is rendered into subsequent, more reflective forms. And that is precisely what makes his work so remarkable: the pain of loss, the bitterness, even the joy – all these things surface seemingly so casually, unintentionally, spontaneously in his poems, whether the occasion is a postcard, a wheelbarrow or a forgotten brand of cigarette. It is in quotidian objects that history becomes momentarily legible in a precise, unrepeatable configuration of the past and the present.

Becker's literary method, his 'journey into the landscape', was shaped from the very beginning by his childhood wartime experiences. Becker's landscapes are spaces across which manoeuvres take place and his texts too are in manoeuvres across many landscapes. Heinrich Böll, once a corporal, was the first to draw attention to this quality in a discussion of Becker's first, much-acclaimed book, *Fields* (1964): 'The title is pictorial, yet it might also, if one transferred it to a grid map, be drawn from the language of the surveyor, or from the language of the strategist . . . Each individual field is entered in the spirit of experimentation, its dimensions noted, and it is then filled with various goods or troops.'

4.

I envisage three prerequisites for the Jürgen Becker poem I imagined during our drive along the old *Panzerplatten* roads in the Darss:

Firstly, a specific location as the medium of the poem, in which it will construct its own space.

Secondly, some kind of familiarity with this place in the past. The imagination needs a point of reference, a connection, in its own history from which to revisit the location. The poem needs this authentic starting point because only then is it 'vouched for', not merely arbitrary, only then can it lay claim to a significance beyond the limitless supply of the theoretically possible.

Thirdly, the process of remembering, backwards and forwards, up to the present which is also experienced 'historically' because, in the poem, it is also an element in the history of the location. And simply remembering one's own past, if it stretches back twenty or fifty years, generates around its historically brief span that powerful, magnetising field within which the narrative can maintain its imperative and its atmosphere, even in the wider spaces that always stand at a distance from time and place. The memory of one's own past authorises our access to history. A literary generation that, more or less smugly, reports it has experienced nothing casts doubt over the nature of its 'former selves'. I would prefer to say that – whatever the situation of this 'former self' – the moment it enters the realm of experience it is nevertheless linked to history and the narratives of the past. However, according to Jürgen Becker's narrator in *The Missing Remainder*, this may be little more than wishful thinking: 'Those born in the future . . . will journey through spaces where the scent of history has drifted away.'

It was, as I have said, on the Baltic coast, on the Darss peninsula, that I first met Jürgen Becker. Schnapps had already been served before we sat down to dinner. The conversation flowed. Over the wild boar, as we ate, there was little talk. After the meal, fresh drinks were served and Becker offered cigarettes from one of the blue and white Gitanes packets that seem to be as essential a part of him as the question he then put to me: 'Well now, Seiler, so what happened next?'

(2003)

IN CASE OF LOSS

PETER HUCHEL'S LIFE LIBRARY AND LAND REGISTRY NOTEBOOK

1. LIFE LIBRARY

To begin with, as I remember it, we stood around rather embarrassed and awkward, with our empty boxes, gazing at the bookshelves in Peter Huchel's study in Staufen. Monica Huchel had already begun to take down bibliophilic treasures and she discussed – sometimes with us, sometimes with herself – those items from the poet's library that were to be returned to the house in Wilhelmshorst. She was quite clear about what she was giving us, but was saying goodbye to the books in her own way, with a few sentences appropriate to each, telling us something of the story of the man who had read them. In the end, what we received into our hands was what might be called a poet's life library, all those books with which Huchel had been intimate for decades, filled with notes, letters, jottings, drawings and drafts of poems.

The selection included the green, tattered volumes of the *Forestry and Hunting Archives of and for Prussia*, which, as a child, Huchel discovered stowed alongside shotguns and handwritten cow charms in his grandfather's rifle cupboard and which he later referred to as the first decisive reading adventure of his life. To the last, Huchel continued to read these already disintegrating volumes, originally published from 1816 to 1819. An envelope inserted as a bookmark is addressed to 'Mr Peter Huchel c/o Embassy House Hotel, London' and carries an October 1974 postmark. Huchel travelled through England on his way to Ireland. At the marked page, in the first part of the 1816 volume, an entry begins, 'On Visiting, Migratory and Resident Birds'. Another entry is titled, 'On the Poisoning of Wolves with Crow's Eyes'. On the inside cover of the book, there are tiny columns of pencil-written numbers: forestry calculations. Also from his grandfather's collection come two dark green, marble-papered, notebook-sized volumes in the 1893–1910 series *The People's Library of Radical Change* (*Volkschriften zur Umwälzung der Geiste*), including anti-religious commentaries on the history of creation and on Feuerbach's philosophy. 'Education makes you free!' is the motto of *Meyer's Penny Library of German Classics for All*, the fifty-fifth volume of which contains 'Bürger's Best Poems' and 'Gellert's Fables'. These are followed into our boxes by: Polybius's *History*, Blaise Pascal's *On Religion* and Huchel's own copy of the Holy Scriptures with annotated passages in the Book of Isaiah and bookmarks still at Psalms 19, 39 and 104. A scrap of newspaper marks the Book of Job, chapters 6–8, which bear the page heading 'Job desolate' in Luther's Bible. Scattered throughout, there are underlinings in pencil: little groups of words ('for it has' or 'and so it') that would appear to be nothing in themselves, yet employed as grammatical hinges in the unfolding development of a poem – to facilitate a slowing down, a speeding up or the introduction of new material – could prove valuable in bringing images to vivid, poetic utterance.

During a short break, there is coffee and conversation about the cats, new specimens of which keep showing up to greet us.

Disappearing now into our boxes are Thomas Aquinas, the writings of Jakob Böhme and a treatise on Marsilius of Padua, the source of Huchel's last cycle of poems, 'The Heretic from Padua'. In the Thomas Aquinas (Question 75: 'Man, the Composition of His Spiritual and Physical Essence'), two questions have been highlighted: 'Is the human soul composed of substance and form?' and 'Is the human soul indestructible?' Huchel would, on occasions, declare Jakob Böhme's *Aurora* to be his favourite book and 'the most beautiful thing the German language can look back upon'. Also densely littered with coloured underlinings and marginal notes is *JU-TAO-FO: the Religious and Philosophical Systems of East Asia* by F. E. A. Krause. A faded, partially erased draft of a poem can be seen in the endpapers of *Universism: the foundations of the religion and ethics, of the political system and science of China* by J. J. M. de Groot: 'The bones rot, breath / rises from the ashes and / becomes light . . .' In his poem, 'Wei Dun and the Old Masters', Huchel transformed this to create the concluding stanza, which went through several revisions during the 1950s:

> The bones rot in the depths.
> Yet breath rises into the air
> And flows as the light through which once,
> O, Old Masters, you walked in great peace.

Concerning the Chinese idea of the dualism of the human soul and its close relationship with the universe, de Groot cites a passage from the Confucian *Book of Rites* which, almost word-for-word, represents the wellspring of Huchel's poetry: 'All living beings must die and that which must return to the earth in death is called *gui*; bones and flesh moulder in the depths and imperceptibly become dust; but breath (*qi*) rises into the air to become radiant light.'

We are back again in the room with the fireplace. Furs are spread over the claw-footed armchairs, and we are told we are sitting where the cats sleep. Monica Huchel had the fireplace installed while her husband was away on a reading tour, but now it lies unused. Newspapers and letters are piled beneath the window. In her invariably confident, occasionally abrupt manner, she directs our conversation from talk of publishers to the cats to the state of her health. Her views are offered firmly, briskly. She feels she has 'had her time' and the idea of witnessing the 'whirl' of celebrations on Huchel's one hundredth birthday horrifies her. She says 'Huchel has . . .' or 'Huchel wanted . . .'; she never says 'my husband'. 'I didn't want to be a mere appendage and there's little room in public beside such a man. Even so, I subordinated myself to Huchel to such an extent that only my almost excessive self-confidence prevented me from losing myself in the process. I know that I would not have done that for any other man.'

To the last, she is doing what she has always done at Huchel's side. She takes care of the things that need to be dealt with. Under her guidance, the house in Wilhelmshorst is being renovated before my family and I move in. In the 1950s, she quickly learned Russian because no one else in the editorial department of *Sinn und Form* spoke the language. She bribed the coalmen so there would be enough fuel to last the winter. For the journal, she translated texts from Fedin to Sholokhov. After Huchel's sacking as editor-in-chief, she provided for the upkeep of the family by taking on further translation work. She managed the arrangements for Huchel's departure to the West and made sure the five hundred books, those we are now sitting in front of and sorting through, were included in those arrangements. For a long time, she nursed the seriously ill Huchel, who died in 1981. In the twenty years that followed and to the end, she took great care of his work and his estate, showing a determination and generosity that is not often thought of as characteristic of 'poets' widows'.

'Now, children, what else could I give you . . .' Hardly pausing in her conversation with the books, Monica Huchel takes down from the shelf a six-hundred-page volume and a postcard falls to the floor: 'A little astronomy for my very dear neighbour . . .' it reads. *The History of Science from St Augustine to Galileo* by A. C. Crombie was a gift from the astronomer Karl-Otto Kiepenheuer. The view of Florence on one side of the card carries the date of Huchel's seventieth birthday. A torn-off ticket (number 53) for the 'Peter Huchel Poetry Reading / Grosser Redoutensaal Passau / 26 July 1973' has been used to mark a page in the philosophy of the thirteenth century: 'Empedocles believed that life arose by spontaneous generation from the earth: first plants appeared and then parts of animals (including man), heads, arms, eyes, etc., which united by chance and produced forms of all sorts, monstrous or proper. The proper forms extinguished the monstrous . . .'

Finally, our survey of the bookshelves arrives at Huchel's own 'reading copies', editions of his collections of poetry as they had accompanied him on reading tours, the last of them in Italy. In the 1972 volume *These Numbered Days* (*Gezählte Tage*) the poem 'Cockscombs' has a slip of paper attached to it which preserves the text in its first impromptu draft and is dated 'Rome, 16 October '71, 2.10 p.m.' The recording of the exact moment suggests a remarkable sense of euphoria. As a rule, Huchel never wrote spontaneous poems, especially those that – as in this case – went on to be published almost unchanged. On page 46 of the same collection, at the poem 'Macbeth', we discover a letter from an English translator named Bill Reed, from Northwood, who is offering polite observations about the poem's translation into English. An advertising leaflet for 'Beaujolais Nouveau 77' has been torn into regular strips to provide further bookmarks for the selection of poems to be read on that last tour. At the end of 1977, in Hamburg, Huchel suffered a stroke. He spent the ensuing years in Staufen.

What is certain is that not all the titles that ought to be assigned as elements of Huchel's 'life library' came to light that afternoon. The library reveals Huchel's efforts to build bridges to the texts of the 'ancients', to a 'childhood of myths'. But here the ancients are not merely a medium for the 'evocation of a mythical archetype' (Walter Jens), or for the creation of a 'private mythology' (Axel Vieregg). In the context of the poet's workshop, such texts often offered concrete materials and patterns of imagery for new poems. Huchel adopted and modified passages from the *Epic of Gilgamesh*, Jakob Böhme, Aquinas, Bachofen, Polybius and the Chinese philosophers for his own writing. As Christoph Meckel has written, in his poem dedicated to Peter Huchel, he panned 'gold from Chinese treasuries'. The style, rhythm, imagery and the 'great peace' of the ancients provided a solid grounding for the historical space in which he found his own voice.

At last, Huchel's complete edition of *Sinn und Form*, bound in half-yearly volumes, also finds its way into our boxes. Now, a quarter of a century after these books accompanied Huchel on his departure from the GDR to the West, the plan is that they will be returned, via the United Parcel Service, to the place from which so many of them had once been seized, thrown into trucks, and then left to rot. Huchel himself saved the most valuable items from this, his abducted archive, when, a few months later, he actually discovered where they had been dumped. Books and correspondence from the journal's editorial team had been simply abandoned in a leaky garden shed, the personal effects of somebody who had died had been piled on top of them. Not only did the *Sinn und Form* volumes themselves have to be recovered: Huchel, an archaeologist of his own work, also had to bring back to the light of day, piece by piece, the letters of Bloch, Brecht, Döblin and Thomas

Mann, or at least as many of them as he could reclaim from that mouldering heap.

Then, all too quickly, it is time for us to be leaving Staufen and a taxi has been called. No visit lasts more than three hours – that is all we have. Then, 'Oh, look, children, here's something else': we are standing, in the midst of our farewells, when Monica Huchel picks out a small yet substantial book, bound in black cloth, with the title 'Notes'.

2. LAND REGISTRY NOTEBOOK

It turns out to be one of Peter Huchel's notebooks, but this is no ordinary collection of poet's notes. When we open it, we find lists of metaphors sorted under particular hieroglyphs and numbered in double-page spreads – a sort of register of spontaneous images that could also function as an organised, retrievable catalogue of images for poems in the process of being written. Listed, one beneath the other, on the left-hand page inside the front cover, are simple line drawings that constitute a table of contents.

The first of these symbols, a semicircle opening downwards, stands for the metaphorical grouping of winter, ice and snow. Beneath that, the second, third and fourth symbols stand for spring, summer and autumn. Beneath these, there is a symbol shaped like a mountain, linking to page 32 of the notebook, and there you find listed hill metaphors, imagery associated with the furrow, the railway embankment, etc. This is followed by a section of bird, flight and sky metaphors. Two parallel wavy lines, linking to page 48, are a clear indication that this section contains all things maritime, notes on water and fish. The sticklike creature sketched beside the number 54 represents the poetry of the lamb, the cow, the sheep, the spider, etc. Beneath this appears an even more cryptic symbol which, judging by the notes in this section, relates to fruit and flowers. At 70, the indicative symbol seems to be that of the plough and here Huchel gathers together a large number of entries on farming, mostly set in the war and post-war periods. This is followed by a circle as the symbol for the lunar, astronomical and earth metaphors that can be found from page 75 onwards. The lightning bolt listed next points us towards page 80 and refers to the element of fire. This is followed by the sickle, under which Huchel has set aside five double pages for other agricultural matters. The list concludes with the symbol of the house, under which Huchel has collected ideas for images associated with domesticity, from the stable in Bethlehem to the 'mortuaries of snow'.

The fundamental principle is this: the poetic raw materials are classified according to the locations in which they appear. Huchel distilled his initial notes not according to theme, but on an almost scenic level. In contrast to the spring and summer pages, the double pages 1 to 8 under the sign of winter are extremely detailed; those familiar with Huchel's poems will not be surprised by this. Nor is it surprising that the pencil notes grow denser again under the sign of autumn, including, on page 24, the almost complete opening stanza of the poem 'Dedication', which was written for Ernst Bloch. Huchel did not only use this notebook for initial ideas, he immediately began to work on the texts, often rearranging words within a line or re-jigging lines within a stanza; a found image was being manoeuvred into a variety of contexts until some usable poetry emerged.

I need to interrupt myself for a moment here, rather than skipping over my own feelings of unease. This notebook, of course, was never intended for publication or for public discussion. Yet its poetic nature and the very clear gesture which put it into my hands have both convinced me that I could not simply allow it to disappear into my own library or be left to languish in some museum display case.

The notebook opens — as I have already said — with the section of winter images and work on a poem about the 'quietest hour', a phrase Huchel used to allude to the birth of Christ. Among these images of winter and snow, most things to be found on these first pages are what even an amateur writer might have done, what might have come to him if he was intent on being 'poetic': the white snow turns blue, it tumbles out of a 'grey mist', the whole scene is set during 'nights of crackling frost', plus a messianic tone: 'Grey sky, snow will fall / in the quietest hour of all . . .' The often remarkable banality of the early stages of a poem will not surprise anyone familiar with such work through their own efforts. Nevertheless, in these notebook pages, Huchel works out the atmosphere of those wintry images which later feature in his well-known winter poems such as 'Winter Psalm' and 'Dedication', poems dedicated to his Marxist friends Hans Mayer and Ernst Bloch, poems which were interpreted as critiques of the political ice age under the Ulbricht regime. Through somewhat more insipid vocabulary and more facile metaphors, the poet writes himself into his own image world. Right from the start, he does not gather together the poem's objects in prose or paraphrase, but rather with metaphors. Starting from the commonplace, Huchel works to elevate his material into poetry.

Huchel's technique is simple. First the essentials are noted: cold, snow, a homecoming, cranes, a ferryboat. Whether the returnee will step across an 'ice-encrusted threshold' or 'plank' or 'bark' is still undecided. At a second or third stage, there are often lines which seem to resemble a cloze exercise. There are two or three completed lines and, following that, lines in which phrase lengths and syntactical constructions are sketched in with commas, rhyme words or the initial words of subordinate clauses. Rhetoric and syntax are, as it were, pre-constructed in this gappy text, whereas the momentum, the tone, the narrative voice, all these are yet to be fixed, are tried out first with 'insipid' vocabulary which is gradually improved, heightened, poetically tempered in a process of replacement. You might say: for the ear, the poem is already complete.

In these initial stages, in his search for material, Huchel works with impressions that often contain something sought-out or precious and which is usually captured with the aid of 'like' comparisons and 'of' metaphoric constructions. From 'the sky red with the setting sun' is developed 'the evening sun like a fire / flaming in a forge' or 'the red carnation of the evening'. Then an improved version, without 'like' and without the participle: 'the evening sun lights / the forge's fire'. This is better crafted, but still not really usable. Yet such an image works like a raw recording which can be worked up later; it preserves something of importance that may still require the passage of time. Perhaps ten or twenty years later, the author can make something of it when re-reading his image notes, because he sees and understands his own experience from that earlier time, to which this vivid impression once belonged. Poems can be constructed of such materials – that have been 'hung for a long time', as they say of meat – even if they involve images of the setting sun like those which Huchel did eventually put to use in poems like 'Roads' or 'Polybius'.

Often, however, it was not the reworkings that entered Huchel's later poems, but straight steals from impromptu notes whose poetic value seems to have been recognised as an immediate gift. For example, the phrase 'The cold cut the teeth' on page 6, re-emerges as an image at the close of the poem 'The Courtroom' ('Cold cut me to the teeth'). Or on page 7: 'They bent the neck of the ram / back and stabbed the knife / into its throat' is an image found in only slightly changed form in the poem 'Farewell to Shepherds'. There is nothing in the contexts of these two notes that gives any clue as to the way they will be later used. But two drafts of letters or statements that happen to appear on some nearby pages prove to be revealing. There, Huchel is revisiting the political arguments about his difficult position as editor-in-chief of *Sinn und Form*. In each case – noted under the symbol of the mountain and that of the house – Huchel defends himself against some of the many attempts to control him: 'So it happened this time too . . . Mr Haid [Bruno Haid, until 1963 head of the publishing department in the Ministry of Culture] . . . came on behalf of Minister Abusch . . . You know the squabbles of propaganda . . . It would be absurd to refer to the human rights laid down in the United Nations Charter . . . it sometimes seems impossible to break this vicious cycle of people endlessly trying to "normalise" their relationships with me, yet without granting me the least rights that any academic would be entitled to . . .' Huchel is here intent on articulating his own position at a time when he was facing growing pressure. In 1963, for example, after Huchel's forced resignation as editor-in-chief of *Sinn und Form*, Politburo member Alfred Kurella tried to dissuade the poet from accepting the (West Berlin) Fontane Prize by observing that he had seen many poets die of false pride. A little later in the notebook, we find bird and sky metaphors, which conclude with the image of snow as 'the grey dragnet of the sky', an image which later forms part of the opening of the poem 'Snow', dedicated to Huchel's friend Hans Henny Jahnn: 'The driving snow / the great dragnet of the sky / it will not catch the dead'.

The poem 'Farewell to Shepherds' – not an outstanding work, but a characteristic text – is a good illustration of Huchel's way of working and how referring to the notebook can help to illuminate it.

'FAREWELL TO SHEPHERDS'

1. Now you are leaving
2. forget the mountain-cool night,
3. forget the shepherds,
4. they bent the ram's neck back
5. and a grey-haired hand
6. thrust the knife into its throat.
7. In a wave of mist
8. the light of first creation
9. swims back again. And beneath the fir tree
10. the never-ending
11. circle of needles and damp.
12. This is your sign. Forget the shepherds.

The image of the 'mountain-cool' in line 2 can be found in the notebook, listed, of course, under the symbol of the mountain, at the start of the section beginning on page 32. The ram image in lines 4–6 appears in the notes under the sign of winter on page 7 of the notebook. The central image of the second stanza, from line 10 onwards, can be found on page 37, also under the sign of the mountain: 'Under the fir tree / a never-ending circle of needles and damp, over which / the compass broke'. Under the symbol for images linked with the moon, the universe and the earth – in other words, with the circle – Huchel jotted down on page 76 a similar image: 'A breath of earth of needles / and wet moss, / the fir trees, the rocks, / they look at you / with the eyes of the dead'. There then follows a more philosophical reflection: 'The never-ending circle of existence, over which the compass broke . . .' Huchel takes up this idea of a 'lost wholeness' from de Groot's book on China – previously referred to –and this is the only entry at odds with the methods of the notebook apart from the letter drafts I mentioned and a few drawings and self-portraits done in ballpoint pen.

Whether wintry or warm, Huchel's skies are most often 'bare' or 'stony grey' and the atmosphere remains the same from text to text; even in his Italian poetry it is often raining. Only some passages in the notebook sound completely unfamiliar, though they are no less interesting for that. Perhaps they are quotations from elsewhere. For example: 'So she stumbled behind me barefoot / driving flies away with a branch'.

So, from four different parts of his finder's logbook, Huchel drew materials for the composition of his short poem, 'Farewell to Shepherds', which he published for the first time in 1971 and then in the 1972 collection *These Numbered Days*. This process of collecting and subsequently assembling poetic raw materials from a wide variety of sources can be illustrated through other examples. Clearly, Huchel never doubted the intrinsic, poetic value of these materials, the validity of which he trusted until the moment when his work on a poem-text would call up from memory the specific image to be used. Scattered throughout the notebook are early drafts and variants of metaphors for subsequent beginnings and endings of poems: 'image-visions not sorted by any theme . . . a few iron filings, as it were, still beyond the magnetic field'. In this brief observation, made by way of self-analysis and prompted by the poet Hilde Domin, Huchel is obviously hinting at his own methods. In the notebook, his shuffling of various contexts and variants reveals the powerful attraction exerted by a metaphor that has been deemed a success – there are repeated efforts to integrate the metaphor into the poem he is working on and which he feels needs strengthening. If it does not succeed on this particular occasion, the search continues for a text in which the image works and the magnet finally organises the iron filings, as Huchel called them.

Every poet drags this secret supply of rough diamonds through the notebooks of his writing life. Some of them take years, possibly decades, to find their right home; the difficulty of placing them is suggestive of their specificity, their particular importance. The inevitably recurring attempts to give these images their text, to accommodate them within the enclosure of a context of meaning, can be extremely productive. New texts are created when one of these images comes into play, even if it does not itself finally work there. Perhaps some are never to be accommodated, some are never to be published; yet they underpin the work from text to text with their restless and continuing existence.

Moreover, almost every page of the notebook contains examples of these 'iron filings' that may later become 'magnetised' to a theme and are familiar in the finished poems. Under the autumn sign on page 25, Huchel sketches three stanzas of a poem:

> And come evening still a mild scent
> the white clouds over the village:

> You take the path
> where sheep leave wool
> hung on the thistle.

The shepherd stands by the house.
The remoteness of the universe
blowing hard into his eye.

Here the tendency to kitsch in the first and third stanzas is hard to deny and Huchel never put lines like these into a finished poem. But they were perhaps important as a kind of mood context for the image in the second stanza which survives and adapts itself to reappear in the poem 'Elegy', published in 1963's *Roads, Roads (Chauseen, Chauseen)*:

Down the path,
where on a thistle
goat's hair blows.

On the notebook pages associated with the signs of the plough and the sickle, Huchel collects a good deal of material for 'The Law', his projected cycle of poems on East German land reform. This is the only grouping that is organised thematically, in the strict sense of the word, and it allows us to date the beginnings of the notebook to the years 1954–1955. Until the mid-1950s, Huchel was working on versions of these poems, one of which appeared in 1956 in the GDR literary journal *Neue Deutsche Literatur*. Probably after that, Huchel abandoned them. He knew the text was unfinished and as yet unsuccessful, but given his growing disillusionment with agricultural policy in the East, he could no longer motivate himself to continue to wrestle with it. Accordingly, many of the images collected for the land reform cycle eventually drifted into quite different poems and metaphors. For example, the final lines ('A generation / eagerly striving / to destroy itself') in the poem 'Psalm', which is the concluding poem in the collection *Roads, Roads*, is extracted from this material. In fact, this line represents

a remarkable revision of the rather melodramatic and optimistic
pitching of the 'Law' material where we read of 'A generation /
striving with all senses / to live happily'. Most of the pencil notes
on these densely covered pages were left unused in the end. This is
often material that seems fundamentally alien to Huchel's diction,
and which was barred by his poetic self-censorship: lines such as,
'But it helps, it helps! / Soon you will be standing in the light /
But you don't know it!' (page 71) or phrases such as 'tractor park'
and 'trailer equipment'. The whole notebook entry shows just how
profoundly Huchel struggled to make land reform in the GDR
a subject for artistic creation. At the same time, it is clear how
restricted his poetic options became the moment he accepted such
a thematic limitation. Christof Siemes has pointed out that in
Huchel's texts the meaning of his natural symbols shifts and often
cannot be pinned down. Huchel's way of working in his notebook
underlines this: a free, flexible depositing of the poetic materials

which later allowed an equally unconstricted access, geared to the demands of whichever text was being worked on at the time.

Jakob Böhme calls the whole of the sensually perceptible qualities of a thing its 'signature'. Huchel was strongly drawn to Böhme's mysticism and his conviction that in humans, animals and plants, outer appearance corresponds to an 'inner form'. Huchel's register of natural phenomena, as found in this remarkable notebook, can easily be read as a system of such 'signatures', according to which he undertook to provide an account of his poetic world. Signature by signature, the poet attempts to make a record of his landscape and with it the essence of things, and hence to transform the whole into language, into 'outer form'. Fourteen signatures to be made use of in the ritual of entering into the symbolic circle of nature, the 'never-ending circle of needles and damp, over which / the compass broke'.

POSTSCRIPT

Huchel moved into his house on Hubertusweg, in Wilhelmshorst, in mid-1954, at which point the notebook was carefully inscribed 'in case of loss'. It is the only book of its kind. Huchel continued to fill his metaphorical storehouse with notes to the very end. Even when he had long since given up residence in the East, in the period following his departure for Rome in 1971, and during his last years in Staufen, the address in the notebook, the one to be sought out – 'in case of loss' – by any discoverer of the mislaid book, the precise location in the landscape from which the notes draw much of their substance, was never altered. And, as if a wish, long buried in the refusal to update the address, was to be fulfilled, the book was now to be returned there, only a few decades later – and without having been lost.

(2003)

AURORA: AN ATTEMPT TO ANSWER THE QUESTION 'WHERE IS THE POEM GOING TODAY?'

1.

Just after seven in the morning, a few hundred metres from my bed, the sounds of construction start up: two jackhammers, pickaxes, shovels, the rumbling of rubble dumped into a skip. At first, each of the sounds is isolated, lost; I'm still half-asleep. But then, though my eyes are still closed, an image of the building site materialises. A shovel lies on the ground, set aside or perhaps discarded, and I think: 'I ought not to have done that.' Somewhere deep in my chest a sense of guilt gathers and declares: 'You have to go back now.' In a moment, the full extent of my predicament dawns. How am I going to explain why I have been absent for so long? Something is telling me: 'Get to your locker, get into your workman's overalls, the hard hat, the folding rule and pencil, stow your civvies on the top shelf.' This really does wake me up. I have a headache and any sense of relief is short-lived. I know this old uprising. The feeling of guilt will eventually subside, but it simply withdraws into its den and, at the next opportunity, it leaps out to re-enact the whole story again.

Staring into the bathroom mirror, I reassure myself that time has passed. I am standing here as a 'Writer', a 'Fellow', in the luxurious villa called Aurora on the outskirts of Los Angeles. I am not here as a 'carpenter' or 'bricklayer' who is, at the behest of one of the millionaires on Pacific Palisades, laying the foundations and formwork for an even better, even larger swimming pool. What that means is: actually, I do not have to rush to my locker. I do not have to get changed quickly, to hurry along the corridor of a bunkhouse – which, moments ago, when I was still half-asleep, seemed to be my only right and proper path. I do not have to run past dormitories from which drift the sickly smells of lukewarm breakfast leftovers, the tang of stale sweat, the reek of last night's booze.

Despite my sense of guilt – for an awful moment rooted in the offence which, during military service in the National People's Army, was termed 'absent without leave' and would always be recorded by the OOD (Officer on Duty) in order then, through further official channels, to trigger the prescribed punishments – I now realise that I do not have to return to my *customary* place. I once read in Martin Heidegger, 'Your origin remains your future' (*Herkunft aber bleibt stets Zukunft*), which struck me as an utterly devastating idea. But it is OK – I had not simply absconded for the past seventeen years. I did not have to think up some absurd story (credible or not, it would still result in weeks of ribbing and ridicule and, in telling it, I would have to bend down, pick up the shovel and get digging to prove I had no illusions about what I ought to be doing, about where I truly belonged). No longer. A quick look at my diary reveals that, these days, I have quite different things to be busy with. For example, before the end of September, I have undertaken to consider the question: 'Where is the poem going today?'

At the age of twenty-one, during my time in the military, I started to read, and at the same time I started to write. Why exactly this happened remains a mystery to me to this day. Before my basic military service, I trained for three years in construction and worked on building sites as a bricklayer and a carpenter for a further three years. Nothing in that period ever suggested poetry. Literature did not interest me. Also, my time in the military might have been occupied in other ways. With fretwork, for example, like the other ten men in my barracks room. That is, with the painstaking creation of complicated plywood scenes, with an endless sawing and sanding of hunters, fir trees and wild animals which, once fully assembled, were the sort of thing that proved popular as Christmas decorations, especially in Thuringia and Saxony: the Schwibbögen (fretworked candle arches), Christmas pyramids (wooden carousels that turn when their candles are lit) and candle holders. I witnessed hundreds of these pieces taking shape, or, more exactly, I heard them taking shape. After I had been discharged, one of the first things I had to adjust to was being able to read a book without the racket of woodworking in the background. Admittedly, I did not completely resist the intoxicating effect of fine wood dust and its scent getting into everything: the bunk beds, the grey metal frames, the underwear carefully stowed in the corners of open lockers. But it never became a thing for me; I never got hooked on it. I finished only one piece, a three-pronged candlestick and, in the course of making it, over several days, I managed to break all my comrades' spare fretsaw blades. It just was not my medium. In these candelabras, for the sake of sturdiness, the neighbouring elements need to be joined – if only via a slight, almost invisible link at their uttermost points. It was exactly in these fragile areas, these hyper-sensitive spots, these wafer-thin bridges – for example, the end of the barrel of a hunter's shotgun linking to the tip of a deer's left ear – where the skill of the one handling the saw was to be demonstrated. I was not conscious of the surreality of all this. It was just as in life: what was most obviously expedient – stability, structure – established the tableau as 'normal', and what appeared normal rendered its surreality quite invisible.

Yet a good ten years later, I wrote poems that had been, in that earlier period, when poetry did not feature in my life, gathering and storing their subject matter, their materials. Doubly hidden from me at the time, clearly the poems had been, even then, making their way towards me. What is different these days is that I have become more conscious of the signs of a poem being on its way. I am aware of what situations, materials and substances it might respond to, what it is likely to ingest – for later use. In my experience, at least seven years can go by before the writing begins. The interval itself seems important here, since only 'with time', with such a minimum of history behind it, do such materials really become of use, properly matured. From this perspective, even *today*, when a poem is in the offing it is just as invisible as it was back then. But it has lost its two-fold invisibility by being roused, for one reason or another, out of unconsciousness. So perhaps I can try to trace it, to contemplate *today* how the poem is on its way for later: 'where the poem is going today'. To do this, I will take at face value the personification of the poem implied in the question; I simply distinguish it, release it from its anonymity. I will call it: the AURORA poem.

2.

The Californian suburban idyll: palm trees, eucalyptus trees, lemons, the lush green of the vegetation, market garden cultivars perfectly suited to the irrigated environment. The lawn at the front of the house feels like rubber underfoot. At midnight, a murmuring begins: the sprinklers have switched on. The neighbourhood dogs are barking a coyote back into the desert. Around two o'clock it grows quiet, then from here we can also hear the Pacific. When I come back late from one of the cinemas in Santa Monica, or Hollywood, the asphalt on the short road that winds up from

Sunset Boulevard towards the villa is wet. At the sides of the road, water runs in little rivulets that are fed from the gardens of the millionaires to left and right. On the dashboard of my car is a remote control for the garage door. From the garages, a door leads directly into the corridor on the upper floor of the house where the bedrooms and studies are located. I have to walk just a few metres, on the same level, and I reach the door of my room. There is a telephone in the room with 'Lion' inscribed beside the number. This was the bedroom of the exiled writer, Lion Feuchtwanger, and it is his bed in which I am now sleeping. In an earlier poem of my own ('living in completed chapters'), I tried to reflect on what it is like as a writer to be living in a dead writer's house, to sit in rooms with the dead. The poem opens with a strikingly austere phrase: 'place of remembrance: stand guard'. Here, in their silent, unrelenting fashion, there are lots of busts keeping watch in every room. Most of them are heads of Martha and Lion Feuchtwanger, set up here in the windows, on shelves, even on the floor, and they remind me of a phrase from Italo Calvino: 'The gaze of the dead is always rather reproachful.' But the AURORA poem is not concerned by that. On the contrary, it likes to walk through an unfamiliar house, the strangeness puts it at ease, gives it focus.

A book lover's residence: distributed in rooms throughout the house, there are 14,000 books, exuding that muted, musty, slightly numbing odour of a memorial library, the most recent acquisitions of which date back fully fifty years and which have hardly been used since. On the bookshelf in the corner stands a basket made of reddish-brown raffia. I lift its close-fitting lid; it contains buttons, thread and a pincushion on which are depicted two Siamese sumo wrestlers, shoulder to shoulder, each with a determined expression, clasping a larger-than-man-sized bale of cloth, ready to be pricked. The thread is not stored on cardboard winders but tiny reels: 50, 60 or 100 yards, *mercerised/boilfast* by J & P Coats. The buttons are red, white, brown and black. They are made of plastic, metal (scratched where they have been polished with steel wool), plus imitations of staghorn, mother of pearl – there is not a single wooden button. To my surprise, I also find a few buttons from a uniform that I cannot identify, the thread eyelets grown a little rusty. That this box of buttons has survived at all is remarkable in view of the museum-like emptiness of the rest of the house; a curious survivor of the household belongings long since dispersed, largely discarded, and almost as strange as the canes, the various walking sticks, I discover in the corner of a small storage room along the corridor. They lean there as if only recently forgotten or, alternatively, left there on purpose by someone calculating they would be close to hand in an emergency. I step out along the corridor, making use of one of the sticks, knocking on the floorboards. I wonder how the return of these noises, silenced since Martha Feuchtwanger's death in 1987, might be interpreted by the staff of the house who occupy the rooms below. In the same moment, I hear my grandmother's voice: 'That's no way to behave.' Only much later did I understand that her reprimand was not so much an expression of ethical concern, more a superstitious outlook that did not want to tempt misfortune. It was probably the same with the walking sticks as with the buttons: what prevented them from being finally disposed of was the intimate connection these objects once had with the body of the deceased, a similar sense of superstition, of consideration, a vague feeling of shame perhaps, as abashed as the walking sticks now gathered in the corner of the storeroom.

Lion Feuchtwanger died in 1958. Martha Feuchtwanger survived her husband by almost thirty years. The sewing kit contained buttons that had accumulated over the course of a lifetime, collected from a variety of eras and fashions, and now they had become irrevocably detached from their fabrics. Looking at them, no one would be able to remember an item of clothing, a specific time, an episode, or anything at all concrete. Yet when the poem makes its way alone through a strange house, it encounters paradox. The things from an unknown past become mementos. When I tip the button box onto the desk (which is said to have once belonged to Franz Werfel), it provides a memory game for the AURORA poem, which acts perhaps like a child playing with buttons, abstracted, engrossed. When it turns up this button, it sees a face that speaks. The poem lays down a path, with figures, pairs of eyes, it creates a story, and it is not about the imagined preciousness of a button but its actual preciousness. The poem also recalls another poem containing the line 'The dead turns up its eye' (Dylan Thomas). Buttons as eyes: the obvious mimicry of a look. The button eyes of home-made dolls and the hypnotic nature of their gaze, or: the sightless, blind nature of their gaze, its potency. In the pupils' place, there are pinprick holes through which the needle travels into the head when the eye is being attached. 'Look deeply into the eyes' we say, and what does this mean? The blind eye lets us gaze deeply, but in a reversed sense: the gaze probes rather into the depths of ourselves and becomes the precise receptacle of our own feelings. This is the most important condition for the intimacy or antipathy a child might experience when playing with a doll. In a bookshop on Fairfax Boulevard, I found a picture book with two hundred so-called *sock monkeys*. From each of these puppets, each with a pair of beady eyes, a different, distinct feeling stares back at us. Modigliani's portraits of women have a similar effect in that their eyes are entirely covered with grey or black paint, virtually 'emptied', which is why the potency of their expression is such a paradox. Perhaps the sewing kit is just such a paradox for the poem. In any case, I sit at the desk with the Feuchtwanger sewing kit, sorting through the buttons. The poem sorts them into pairs of eyes, it pushes eyes into pairs, it assembles and positions them like utterances on the table. The table now has eyes. I can imagine that it is observing me as I am observing it. I can imagine it contemplating what in me reminds it of itself, etc. In the military button eyes, a propeller is spinning, and beyond it the outstretched wings of a large bird.

The AURORA poem moves on through the house and is look-ing to engage with things. Its powers of illumination are derived from the idea of encouraging these things to speak, before perhaps moving on to connect them with other materials drawn from memory. It would like to become a thing itself, to participate in the conversations between things. A further paradox: the poem is drawn to things that are of a similar substance to itself. In Plato's theory of gravity, the falling and rising of bodies is explained by the assumption that bodies of the same nature strive to converge. So, a stone falls to earth, fire rises to heaven. Here, my poem is responding to buttons and to walking sticks; it is looking for the raw, un-museumised remnants of an earlier era in this house where I am going to live for the next three months – with them it can speak.

3.

A few cardboard and wooden boxes are stacked in the organ cham-ber, which is hidden away behind wall panelling at the far end of the ballroom. The organ, made by the 'Artcraft Organ Company Santa Monica', has been out of action for a long time. Hanns Eisler is said to have played 'Üb' immer Treu und Redlichkeit' ('Be Always Loyal and Honest') on this instrument when the 'New Weimar' of the Californian exiles gathered at the Feuchtwangers' – Heinrich Mann, Thomas Mann, Brecht, Kurt Weill, Alfred Döblin, Franz Werfel, Charlie Chaplin, Billy Wilder, Bruno Frank, Ludwig Marcuse, Albert Einstein, Arnold Schönberg. There are also gramophone records covered with a reddish-brown layer of dirt as if they had once been drowned. Among them are spoken recordings and rare acoustic recordings, such as a record made by Electro-Vox, a recording of the 'Galileo Scene' in Brecht's *Life of Galileo* as it was recorded in the Electro-Vox Recording Studios, Los Angeles on 13 October 1947. Just three days after this recording, Brecht left Santa Monica and, soon after that, left the USA. Some of the records are broken. The black shards remind the poem of a childhood in which the pieces of a smashed spoken recording were treasured for a long time, considered valuable, because there were voices on them, something living that could never be treated as mere refuse. A record that got broken was painful in a way that went beyond simple loss. In the hand, the records from Soundcraft weigh as heavy as roof slates; it is impossible to tell what they preserve. They are labelled with a wax crayon, but only with numbers, and the index to them is nowhere to be found in the boxes. These old records were manufactured from slate dust, soot and shellac, the kind of marriage of voice and substance that the poem's imagination cannot better. Several unusual things lie among the boxes of this neglected sound archive. Among them, there are three identical tie boxes from Wm Chelsea Ltd of New York. The contents of these beige boxes, greying at the edges, are untouched and still folded neatly in their layers of tissue paper. A tiny signature makes a subtle pattern that covers the wine-red fabric. Beneath the three ties are more stacks of records, most of them from the series 'New German Folksongs' by Johannes R. Becher and Hanns Eisler. Clearly, their names have been stamped onto the inside label by the manufacturer at a later date. It is possible that the producers were initially taken in by the title; it is possible they knew of Becher's own statement, quoted everywhere: 'Giving the people a song – what higher calling for a poet? To enter the people as a nameless person, to be carried along by them like a song: that is true fame, that is immortality.' But then, seemingly at the last minute, there seem to have been reasons to prefer – to that sort of immortality – a blue stamp with the abbreviation 'Becher/Eisler'. Those who have not, as I did in former times, stoutly sung these 'nameless' songs from the past, can discover – in the semi-darkness of the organ chamber, with the dust of past decades and its musty Cold War smell in their lungs – that 'folk songs' like the 'Song of Learning' or the 'Song of the Blue Flag' are very much products of authorship. The next find in my rummaging among the voices: a large cardboard sleeve with the handwritten note: 'Recording of Ronald Reagan's Campaign Speech for Governor of California 1965'. The sleeve is empty, unfortunately, no longer enclosing the record. While I am wondering how Arnold Schwarzenegger's Campaign Speech (the election campaign has just begun) might have fitted into this sound archive (between the Intermezzo and the final chorus of the cantata *Middle of the Century* (Becher/Eisler), for example), an almost disintegrating bundle of maps comes to hand. Under a wooden box with at least forty Eterna records from the series 'Song of Time', produced in Otto Stahmann's TEMPO recording studio, Potsdam-Babelsberg, and despatched as a gift from Berlin (postmarked 20 April 1953) and addressed to Dr Lion Feuchtwanger / Pacific Palisades, there is an *Atlas of the World at War* from Matthews-Northrup. It bears the subheading: 'Follow every battlefront of the war on 32 large, richly coloured maps'. On the back of it is an appeal from President Roosevelt, evidently quoted for promotional purposes: 'Look at your map!' Though with a delay of close to sixty years, I now follow Roosevelt's advice and it pays off immediately. From the appendix to the map section, under the heading 'Insignia of the US Army', the unfamiliar military eye-buttons are staring back at the poem, displaying the caption 'Air Corps'. Beside it, an explanatory note: 'The Air Corps consists of pursuit and fighter planes, observation planes and bombers.' And then the poem starts to tell me the beginnings of a brief, simple story to help me remember some of the things it has encountered here:

4.

The story goes that the young writer, James Salter, visited the Feuchtwangers' house in Pacific Palisades in 1953, while on the West Coast on manoeuvres with his squadron. Salter is wearing his Air Force uniform and has a rather embarrassing gift from his hometown, New York: three identical wine-red ties that Feuchtwanger finds acceptable but his wife considers appalling. A stalemate that means the ties remain unworn, but nor are they thrown away. The young Salter talks of his exploits as a fighter pilot in Korea and asks Feuchtwanger to read a manuscript that he says is *set in Europe*. Feuchtwanger cannot wholly dismiss a sense of irritation that seems to stem from the presence of the uniform. But he makes an effort and talks about a fundraising campaign for war bonds among those living in exile; that the proceeds have been used to buy a fighter plane which was christened 'Loyalty' and then presented to the US Air Force. Salter listens patiently. He respects this man who has succeeded in making a living as a writer. Feuchtwanger says he is too tired to return to Europe; he just wants to write, to walk, to look after his turtles. Salter talks about Germany, his squadron, the airfields at Hahn, Wiesbaden, Fürstenfeldbruck. His German has a Bavarian accent. Touched by this, Martha Feuchtwanger steers the conversation towards Munich: the Café Odeon in the Hofgarten, you know, is it still there? Feuchtwanger describes how a little man from the next table – his name was Adolf Hitler – once held his coat there. They are sitting out on the Aurora balcony, the lights winking on across Santa Monica Bay, music coming from the automated organ in the hall. By way of farewell, Salter asks about the name of the villa – whether it refers to the armoured Russian cruiser of the same name . . . Feuchtwanger laughs, grows quiet, and bids him goodbye.

James Salter has not been in touch since then. In 1957, Martha Feuchtwanger cut the buttons off Salter's uniform jacket (the evening had been warm and Salter had forgotten to pick it up). Over the years, she had kept the garment but then she had read in the *Los Angeles Times* that Salter's first novel had been published and that he had left the Air Force. She takes the jacket out of the storeroom beneath the garages and does what was perfectly proper for housewives of her generation and natural for her as the daughter of a haberdasher: using a razor blade, she cuts the buttons from the material before the jacket eventually disappears into a bag of rags. Buttons always have a use, good for later, good for the story the poem is telling me here, because in any present moment the poem is making its way: it is searching for a past for the moment of its own creation. The object of its fascination: that time passes.

(2004)

Today, when I want to drive back to where I grew up as a child, there are many new routes. For example, there is exit 59 on the A4, which I always refer to as 'Gera (East)', though on the road maps it has been given a different name. While even medium-sized towns elsewhere compete to appear on a sign on the autobahn, the small village of my childhood – the 'indomitable' one I'd like to call it, following Asterix – has actually achieved it. The village itself has a population of 502 and is called Korbussen, a name that in my younger years proved painfully difficult for me to pronounce loud and clear in front of my football friends from nearby Gera because -*bussen* sounds very like *Busen* – German for 'bosom'. At that time, the village's name was thought to hark back to the Slavic basket makers who had settled close to the willow trees growing along the Sprotte, still a small stream here, not far-distant from its source. The low ground along the Sprotte always remained sufficiently damp in those days. With the uranium mining of the 1980s, the groundwater sank without trace and along with it went most of the willows. 'The municipal coat of arms shows . . . a black-barked, uprooted willow tree with green leaves; beneath it, on a green ground, a golden handbasket' – so states the municipality's charter.

In her day, my mother still used to cut willow rods. The farm had its own willow stand in a small, marshy, low-lying area. It grew in a field a good way from where we lived, on a twenty-by-twenty-metre patch of land that was still part of the farm and which we called the 'wood field'. The willow rods she cut would be taken to the basket maker, Schilling, who lived in the neighbouring village of Grossenstein. Schilling produced baskets for potato picking, apple picking, egg collecting, plus bigger baskets used to transport chopped fodder. Also, there were even larger, so-called 'chaff baskets' that were slung across your back. When I was a two-year-old, while my mother was busy milking the cows, she would stand me up in one of these chaff baskets between the rows of stalls. The basket was liable to topple over if I wriggled too much. After I had rolled once through the filthy slurry running down the middle of the milking parlour, I got the message and made every effort to keep still and wait.

On the other side of the A4 stand the suburbs of Gera. Gera-Leumnitz, which is there alongside Korbussen on the exit sign at junction 59, has an airfield that extends right up to the edge of the autobahn. 'Our air force,' my grandfather liked to joke, while making hay and pointing at the sky with his scythe, as one of the old prop planes circled above the fields and disgorged young people who were practising parachuting, 'to defend the peace'. Further to the north-west, you cross several rolling hills that I still, as they say, have 'in my legs' from ski hikes undertaken in my schooldays. We had been living in Korbussen for a few years, but it was already the second village of my childhood. The first, named Culmitzsch, had been demolished to clear more ground for the uranium mines and before we, like many of the villagers who had been evicted, were allocated one of the then much-coveted new apartments in the town of Gera, Korbussen was our home. It took four or five hours by ski to get to Gera-Langenberg. There was nothing remarkable on this route besides the big, curved expanses of snow and, in between, one or two small, cobbled stretches across which wooden skis grumbled pleasingly. By the 1980s, the area was already much changed. A major house-building programme had been declared and prefabricated buildings crawled across the hillsides from Gera-Bieblach towards the villages. This contradicted a story that Gera people like to tell: following the war, when Berlin's four-power status was still being taken seriously, there had been – or so it was said – discussions 'right at the top' that proposed establishing Gera as the new capital of a country that was expected to be reunited in the near future. It was claimed that Gera was a very likely candidate and we all believed it. Apparently, it was only because of 'experts' raising concerns about its geographical location in an unpromising valley basin – something that would have hindered the anticipated expansion of the future city – that these plans were eventually dropped. The pan-German geography, within which Gera might have become a more or less central location, in the end rapidly lost its importance. Gera became merely the 'district capital'. After the opening of the border in 1989, the people of Gera immediately remembered how quickly they could get to the West German town of Hof to do their shopping and that they lived really no more than a stone's throw from Bayreuth.

If I tried to follow our old ski trail nowadays, the one connecting my childhood village to the town, it would not be possible. The blocks of flats of the 1980s and the terraced houses of the post-reunification period had already encroached on Trebnitz, Korbussen's neighbouring village, which once lay halfway across the fields and has now become absorbed into the outskirts of Gera. In Trebnitz could be found the baker who was famed across the whole region for his cream cakes. On every birthday, there was a Trebnitz cream cake, white or brown (if 'real cocoa' was available), with a beautifully decorated number for your age, and lines traced in the icing for sixteen very thin slices. You had to order well in advance and were considered fortunate if your name was listed on the Behr Bakery's small, battered cake calendar which always hung on a string to the left of the cash register. And though I liked cream icing less and less as I grew older, and later could hardly stomach the stuff, those birthday cakes were always received with great excitement and declared delicious: on the special day, as it was lifted from the fridge, a magical aura of custom and remembrance seemed to surround what was in essence an unbearably sweet treat.

Even before our ski trail reached Trebnitz, it had to cross the fields beyond the Grape Vine Tavern, though only the name of the place survived even at that time. Rather than the inn itself, there was an old brickyard and a clay pit, which later dwindled further still to become no more than a small pond with a few fishermen dotted round it. Diagonally opposite the Grape Vine Tavern (a bus stop on the route to Ronneburg had been given the name and so it was handed down), there now stands a Globus hypermarket. Opposite the Globus store lies the old airfield. These days, executives from companies that have established themselves in the area fly in on their private planes. Many of them then simply have to join the autobahn in the direction of Korbussen, using exit 59 – 'Gera (East)' – or, alternatively, they might take the large roundabout which, in more recent times, has been built over the location of the Grape Vine Tavern and, from there, they can gain direct access to the new industrial estate with the traditional sounding name of Korbwiesen ('Wickermead').

For me, it was strange and disconcerting that a sign bearing the name 'Korbussen' should suddenly make an appearance beside the autobahn. In my imagination, the village had always been remote, in all senses, and had nothing to do with autobahns. The new autobahn exit seemed to me to represent the final obliteration of the kind of extraterritoriality that one goes on attributing to the favoured places of childhood, even when the grounds for doing so no longer exist. Of course, I understood the village was not an island even back then. Nevertheless, it was difficult for me to drive along these new roads, particularly because, as I could see, they struck across a landscape that had once belonged to my family and, until 'collectivisation', had been farmed by my grandfather, Erich König. I was born at a time when my mother could still be found labouring in these fields, helping to bring in the harvest. She was adept in the best methods of loading the harvest wagon. Now there are tile markets and car suppliers on the spot where she worked. The Wickermead industrial estate, located on the autobahn exit, is a great success and almost fully occupied – an exception among the ruins of other investments along the East German autobahns and other major roads, all initiated once with much local government optimism.

Loading the harvest wagon is a real art. As in construction, you begin at the corners, laying sheaves alternately from there, in both directions, bound together in an interlocking pattern. The ears are laid in rows towards the middle so that the stack increases in height in a gradual conical shape and to prevent any of the sheaves (that have already been bound with twine by the machine) from 'shooting out', gradually working themselves loose on the journey along the farm track to the barn. As the wagon bringing the tall load turned into the farmyard, my mother would always be assured of her grandfather Edwin's acclaim: 'O my gurl, you's dun it again!'

Anyone who wants to take a last look at the uranium mining district in this area needs to hurry. All the spoil heaps are scheduled for removal by 2007, by which time the German Garden Show will have covered everything remaining with a layer of good dark topsoil. Already, the landscape is undergoing a transformation as forty thousand tonnes of waste material are being trucked out on a daily basis. These days it is recommended that visitors take the so-called 'Regeneration Trail No. 5', which has all kinds of things to offer along its eleven-kilometre circular route. From the viewing platform at the edge of the Lichtenberg open-cast mine, you can let your gaze drift hundreds of metres down into its depths. Or you can hike along the *Panzerplatten* trails, the concrete-slab roads where tanks once manoeuvred, around the foot of the two cone-shaped mountains visible from a distance and, for so long now, the distinctive features of the landscape. Of course, a tourist exhibition mine has been constructed: the real tunnels, which extend over more than a thousand kilometres underground, are sealed off because of radiation hazard. And where the original Ronneburg spa, with its radiant, healing waters, had been discovered in 1666, there is now a glass pavilion to welcome visitors. However, the spring itself disappeared during the mining era and has yet to make a reappearance despite a visible rise in the groundwater in the excavated, abandoned pits.

Junction 59 opened in 1996 with the aim of providing 'improved access' to the Wickermead industrial estate. But actually, this turn-off had always existed unofficially. Without ceremony, you swerved to the right once you had passed under the autobahn bridge, then straight out onto an open field, and from the field onto the paved road that joins Korbussen and Gera. Back then there were no crash barriers. On a Friday evening, my father made use of this shortcut on his ES 250 motorbike when he came back from the Workers' and Farmers' College in Jena and, later, when returning from his studies in Chemnitz, and only with his arrival would the family weekend get under way. This often involved, if the weather permitted, a Sunday excursion out of the village to the edge of the autobahn, a couple of kilometres away. I usually sat in a handcart (or in winter on a sledge) with a blanket folded behind me and our most prized possession, the portable radio, on my knees. It was a Stern-brand radio (*Stern* meaning 'star') with a black leather cover that protected the wooden housing and there was a golden grille over the speaker. At the back of the case, there was a small panel that had to be opened every so often to install two new square batteries. Until I was eleven, this was our main connection to the world, until 1974 when, on the occasion of the upcoming World Cup, my father purchased the family's first television set.

On the embankment close to the autobahn bridge, there were a few birch trees where we would sit and rest. Every car that passed by – and that did not happen very often – was remarked upon. I was supposed to hazard a guess as to the make or model of the car – something that was possible in fact, even for a four-year-old, because of the limited options. Particular highlights were provided by the 'Western cars'. Whoever first saw one of these uttered a swift shout to get everybody's attention, so earning the honour of discovery. On a good afternoon, there were perhaps three or four of these and, in those cases, it was up to my father to guess the make. Sometimes he would sit a little apart from us and closer to the road. I noticed he had made a small cotton-wool ball, and when a car approached our picnic spot, he pressed it into his ear, sometimes only briefly, sometimes for longer. I think he identified the engines in this way, from the sound they made, and he could guess the models of the Western cars without even seeing them. My father knew everything about engines. He had studied mechanical engineering, though at the end of the 1960s he began to write systems programmes for the new mainframe computers at the Gera Data Processing Centre and, later, he would go on to teach computer languages with wonderful names such as Oracle.

It was only much later that I understood these trips across the fields to the edge of the autobahn were manifestations of a longing, a wanderlust that, for my parents, signified an escape from the village, an escape from the farm. Besides this, there was the dream of actually owning their own car – for so long a utopian dream, it came true in the early 1970s when they bought a WAS 2101, which was called a Zhiguli at the time, though later the make was rebranded as Lada. It was a solidly made, angular, snow-white car, manufactured in the Volga.

Early on – even before we moved into town, perhaps during those early excursions to sit beside the autobahn – a sense of longing arose in me too, though in the opposite direction. While the journey out attracted my parents, the A4 between Ronneburg and Gera pointing to their escape route, in my case it was the journey back that was being laid down. Today, when I drive that way along the autobahn and I glimpse the village on the horizon – the tall barns on its perimeter, the slate-tiled church tower, the four or five visible Peace Oaks, one of which, Eduard König, my grandfather's grandfather, planted on the driveway to the farm in 1871, and which his grandson, Erich, had planned to fell one hundred years later with the intention of selling the wood to the furniture industry and was only prevented from doing so by the united opposition of the family – so today, when I catch sight of this little, timber-framed Thuringian village coming into view across the fields, I feel like pulling over, like turning back, 'going home'. With my own children sat in the handcart perhaps, though even they have long since grown up and the village of my childhood is only what it once was when glimpsed from a distance, from the autobahn and in passing.

(2003)

I AM TIRED

before sleep softly I spoke to
my mother's hairpiece I
can't remember how

it sang from its pale
head of styrofoam so softly
songs of lorelei it sang

once more you must be
twenty & it said
I should be asleep[2]

The two villages in eastern Thuringia where I grew up were commonly referred to as the 'tired villages'. It was said that the people who lived there seemed phlegmatic and listless and they themselves complained of a persistent tiredness and they wondered at their absent moments. There was a heaviness that hung over everything, all through the seemingly endless procession of our days on the farm, in the garden and in the maze of outbuildings on what was a moribund estate in the wake of collectivisation. There was a large four-sided farm building around a courtyard, with fodder sheds, washhouses, garages, stables, barns for hay where unused wagons stood and, alongside them, a threshing machine, five metres high that, when set going, made deafening, demonic noises that were enough for me to imagine being summoned into its hopper and ground to pieces. All over the place, there were pools of slurry or standing water that, as a child, you were likely to fall into, if only because of the number of earnest warnings not to do so.

There was something in the atmosphere of these villages. It was as if the swing, rigged up in a tree, and even the garden gate – when you pushed it open to reach the fields at the back – could only move sluggishly through the air. In the heart of the garden, at the very centre of that time, there stood – surrounded by the elaborate circles of my daydreaming – a hut, a self-built shed made of scavenged boards, roofing felt and perhaps a kilo of nails. This was my castle, the most remote outpost of my fiercely contested, fanciful homeland, far out over the steppes, even on occasions standing in the middle of a 'desert'. There I sat and dreamed my favourite dream: heavily armed attacks by foreign superpowers, followed by my own heroic defensive combat until, eventually, the counteroffensive. Most of the time, I led a couple of mounted battalions. Some of them pulled behind them those dreadful little wagons on which sat men who had already lost limbs in battle yet they continued to fire left and right from mounted machine guns. Reports had it that these were the most dangerous and determined of fighters . . . I do not remember where these ideas came from – probably from school, perhaps from a storybook with an illustration of Budyonny's Red Cavalry. At the time, I was mystified as to why such heroes had to wear such ludicrous caps with long, floppy earflaps and pointy tops. When peace broke out across the steppes, I would emulate the exploits of Daniel Boone or Bruce Lee. I would stock up on reserves, establishing hideouts with supplies of lemonade that would ferment within three days.

A peculiar mountain range bordered the world of the tired villages and defined the horizons of my childhood: the spoil heaps and tailing ponds beneath which lay the ore, uranium. When the American occupiers withdrew from Thuringia in 1945 in exchange for the partitioning of Berlin, they had overlooked something: pitchblende lay in the ground, black and glossy as meconium – the cryptocrystalline form of uranium rock, the heaviest of the natural elements. Curiously, these East German deposits had been forgotten by the Western Allies. James Francis Byrnes, the American Secretary of State at the time, declared the Soviet Union would not be able to manufacture atomic bombs simply because there was no uranium to be found in Russia. As soon as the Americans left in 1945, Russian geologists were already surveying the East German uranium deposits. Soon after, the only Communist share corporation on German soil, the Soviet-German company Wismut, started extracting fissile material from the ground for use by the Russians. The American atomic bomb monopoly had been broken.

In the seventeenth century, people had already begun bathing in the strangely pleasant and inexplicably relaxing miracle springs to be found where the barbed-wired, ring-fenced spoil sites now stand. Patients brought their illnesses to the spa: Duke Friedrich III of Saxe-Gotha was treated there for his gout. Then, only three hundred years later, the magical secret of these springs, their radio-activity, was discovered. Yet this did not diminish the business of the spa. On the contrary, radium baths sprang up like mushrooms, radium soap was sold and, on the labels of bottles of drinking water from the state mineral springs of Bad Ronneburg, Professor Schiffner assured their purchasers of 'radioactivity and analysis'. As late as 1916, the medical journal *Radium* claimed that 'radium 14 has absolutely no toxic effects and is absorbed by the human organism as easily as sunlight is absorbed by plants.'[3] Radium treatments flooded the market. Radioactive belts were sold to be strapped to the particular part of the body in need of treatment and there was the 'radium ear', a hearing aid containing the fabulous ingredient 'Hörium'. Likewise, radioactive toothpaste was all the rage, promising its users cleaner teeth and better digestion, and there were radioactive face creams too, supposed to lighten the skin, plus a multitude of other products of dubious efficacy. In 1932, Frederick Godfrey, a British hair specialist, announced 'one of the most important scientific achievements of recent years': a radioactive hair tonic. A chocolate bar both laced with and called 'Radium' and claiming to have rejuvenating qualities was sold throughout Germany.

In short, the famous spa town of Ronneburg, with its sparkling waters, drew an illustrious clientele from across the Empire. My great-grandfather, Edwin König, the last undisturbed farmer in the countryside around Ronneburg (he owned the land he worked), was a frequent visitor to the town. From where autobahn exit 59 and the Wickermead industrial estate are today located, he would set out on a Sunday, acting the grand landowner, on one of his beloved horses, to attend equestrian events or musical events at the spa itself or merely to drink a beer in town and watch the exotic 'foreigners' and the gout-stricken aristocrats as they passed by.

In the twentieth century the marvellous story of the uranium balm came to an end. After the First World War, Bad Ronneburg reverted to plain Ronneburg once more and, following the Second World War, became Ronneburg Mine, along with its cone-shaped slag heaps, tall enough to be visible from a great distance. It was these uranium dumps, their ash-grey effluvia, the thin growths of birch clustering at the foot of their slopes, that became part of my childhood horizon as for other people, perhaps, a nearby mountain range might have done, or merely the ridgeline of the row of houses across the street. When I kicked around out the back or swung on the gate that opened onto the fields, it was their skyline that thrust itself into my daydreams.

Under the command of the Soviet army, the extraction of the uranium ore proceeded swiftly, and with merciless disregard for all affected. My father tells me a drilling rig appeared one morning in our family's garden. One of the neighbours said: 'There's one at our house as well.' Around the same time, the road to one of the neighbouring villages vanished, dug and bulldozed away. East Germany became the third largest uranium mining region in the world (after the USA and Canada), at times employing more than one hundred thousand people. Those who laboured in the mines had to endure long shifts, but they were well paid, had shorter wait times if buying a car, and there was a monthly ration of four bottles of tax-free schnapps: a 0.7 litre bottle for 1.17 marks. The workers dubbed it 'Pitman's Death'. Their style of humour was grim and rose from a mix of knowledge and cluelessness. When my grandfather, Gerhard Seiler from Culmitzsch, returned home from the mine in the morning, we would all still be sitting in the kitchen, listening to the radio. He would come over to us and waft his hand above the wooden box of the receiver. Instantly the music faded into an otherworldly crackling and hissing. When he took his hand away from the box, the haunting subsided and Bavarian Radio could once more be heard. We were impressed and he would laugh. Though I also remember more disconcerting feelings, in the face of such invisible forces, when my grandfather would lay his hand affectionately on top of my head.

The qualities that characterised this period were absence, tiredness and heaviness: these were the states of perception in my childhood that later functioned as the correlatives through which the world was experienced most immediately. This is how such states then become textual qualities, pre-poetic principles, you might say, laid down in childhood. The homeland as a direction of motion – in verse too: 'each poem moves slowly / from above to below . . .'⁴ – towards the raw material, the ore, towards what in age-old miners' lore is called the bones of the earth. Invisible, lost in the depths, down there, lay a region that was unearthed before our very eyes to form that landscape of piled slag, or it was pumped away as slurry. 'A world under the compulsion of the divining rod from Antarctica to the Erzgebirge: uranium, pitchblende, isotope 235! Far-reaching neurosis!' Gottfried Benn's novella *Ptolemy's Disciple* (*Der Ptolemäer*) was written in 1947, just as the German uranium industry was excavating the first of what would end up being 220,000 tonnes of uranium. Subsequently, 500 million tonnes of radioactive waste were left behind in East Germany.

But to those of us who inhabited the place, the sight of the spoil heaps suggested nothing of either compulsion or neurosis. Only at night, pressing your ear to the bedstead, would you imagine you could hear something going on underground; perhaps the kind of thing Büchner's Woyzeck might have heard, a pounding in the earth: 'It's all hollow down there.' I often heard observations of this kind after the water in the pond in front of our house suddenly drained away and it was then rumoured that Wismut had actually begun excavating beneath our village in its quest for new veins of ore. I remember the strange feeling, under the soles of my feet, of treading on thin ground.

Back in the farmyard, I kept myself occupied with objects, with things: dreaming of them, sweating over them, above all talking to them – an endless muttering of dramatic action, monologue, reflection, spoken aloud into thin air. Things changed once they had been taken up into the flow of speech: then, they revealed their unique qualities. So it might be that, as I was working with a piece of wood such as a fence lath, I would be talking all the time or, to be more precise, I would be directly addressing the wood. I would move close to it and talk, touching it with my hands, I would rest my forehead on the lath's rough surface. As a child, I developed a linguistic as well as a physical feel for things like wood. Francis Ponge, in his 'Introduction to the Pebble', sets out a linguistic aesthetic which is at the same time a doctrine of things and a cosmogony: 'The whole secret of an observer's happiness lies in his refusal to consider the intrusion of things into his personality *as an evil.*'

The fact is that my memories of that period consist largely of sounds, things, materials. If such a thing is possible, I would say that my origins were embedded in yesterday's object-world: an abandoned horse sleigh from the landowning era, a dozen bridles, horse-collars, halters, whips and scythe blades hanging on the wall, a last, slow, practically dead horse called Liese, a collection of large and small paraffin lamps, the cellar, the basement storeroom, twenty kinds of cakes on cake boards on a shelf, a butter churn, a boiler, the first electric water pump, the first television set, the Stassfurt television cabinet, with its lamp in the form of Columbus's ship, the *Santa Maria*, perched on top of it. In the glass cabinet, there are a few glittering minerals, beautiful, shiny souvenirs smuggled up from underground and sometimes presented as gifts – the green malachite, the azurite, the ores of cobalt, the raw material for sodalite or 'true blue'. There was also the uneven stone floor in the utility kitchen and, up above, hooks secured to the ceiling's central beam from which animals were hung to be butchered and gutted, the entrails spilled over the kitchen table. The animals would be dragged from the barn at three in the morning: the panic-stricken creatures, the men tugging the 'sow rope' knotted round the pig's ankles. The animals knew straight away what was about to happen and fought for their lives. As the butcher applied the bolt gun to the animal's temple, I desperately gripped its twitching rump and scrabbling legs while my mother held an enamel bowl to the bolt wound, whisking the blood as it spurted out to prevent clotting. Then, the usual quarrel over who should have the brain this time (eating brains makes you clever, we said back then), then the brain in the pan, the smell of it, even as the butchering proceeded, from meat to sausage to schnapps and then the washing of blood from our boots in the evening.

What absolutely did not characterise our lives at this time was a lively sociability. No one around the table had to seek out moments to relax, to reflect, to 'go within'. You were already 'within'. Talk that did occur often did not really seem intended to function as any kind of exchange. What was spoken fell, as if from a great distance, on the ears of those sunk in their own weariness – a contact call, like those emitted by large mammals underwater to mark their relative positions to one another. So no one was ever really alone. And yet tiredness operated as a kind of refuge. You were with yourself and with things, yet without comprehending them particularly clearly, but also closed off, as it were, on the outside of life. It now seems to me, in this state of weariness (a word Goethe uses in *The Sorrows of Young Werther*), there grew up a special and natural intimacy with objects, a sense of hidden kinship. The conventionally assumed duality of subject and object was daily confounded in childhood. I suspect it was precisely this that contributed to the difficulties I had (problems that later grew to torment me) in summarily taking an object for granted, and from there, speaking or writing *on* it. I never felt able to make such a presumption, even though the terms of language encouraged it. My brief career as a doctoral student in literary studies also suffered from similar difficulties. After concluding my studies, I spent a whole two years trying to clarify for myself the terms of my own thinking; the very object of study had to be painstakingly established. Even today, when I think of it, the process seems to resemble nothing so much as an excavation, unearthing an enemy placement, a counter-position from which I am held at bay. In German, 'object' is *Gegenstand*, something that stands counter to you, opposing or against you. At some stage, I gave up the struggle. Like Paul Valéry's Monsieur Teste, I was more inclined to drift off to sleep: 'Sleep will pursue any idea further, whatever its nature.'

After that it was only a short while before my 'object of study' began to fade and then quite disappear. Grown tired and abstracted, I recognised something in things that was familiar to me, something beyond their mere terms and labels, something from long ago.

Perhaps the only thing left to me was to pursue the trade I had learned as a young man (as bricklayer, as construction worker) and, in so doing, I would be earning the kind of honest fatigue that would most likely relieve me of all such abstruse difficulties. On the other hand, I could set out to find a language fit for the peculiarly diffuse nature of my own perceptions.

So much for how it all began.

When I started writing, I conceived of a kind of 'dictionary of diffuse existence' gradually developing into a lexically arranged poetics, organised on the basis of 'particular categories' such as 'absence', 'tiredness' and 'heaviness'. Much of this has since lost its meaning, but some elements of it are still significant for my writing today.

'Absence': I was fascinated by moments of absence in the language of a poem. That is, absence as a looked-for state, the opportunity, as it were, to step back as an observer, to try to perceive things without design, rather than judging them in the light of preconceptions. A state of composure in which poems would yield to that moment of stillness during which it becomes possible to set words and things to one side and, equally, to be left alone by them. Everything then has to do with this utopian ideal of perception – for example, the relationship between movement and stasis, the struggle to propel the movement in a poem towards a grotesque climax, the point at which it attains stillness, and in a moment a wave of 'absence' is set free.

A second category was to be labelled 'heaviness': texts that focused on matter, on substance, on materiality and hence on the weight of things. But weight not only as the attribute of an object, but also in the linguistic expression of such things, in the sense of statements being possessed of gravitational fields that interact one with another. Working on a poem, then, it would be a matter of feeling out and rendering the gravitational pull resulting from such a quality of weight (in this sense) as a barely perceptible mechanism for dealing with such things. Postmodernism, with its infatuation with lightness, flickering, rapidity and flight, has primarily worked on and favoured the dematerialising of ideas. In Joseph Hanimann's *On Heaviness* (*Vom Schweren*) we find a second, contrasting form of modernism which goes a long way to rediscovering this long-neglected sense of weight (the slow, the tired, the cumbersome, etc.) as an essential quality of things and hence of existence itself. So, Hanimann argues, it would then become possible, 'in the ongoing cycle of meaning, of data flows that can be retrieved and stored, to look beyond bodies of simple materiality and hence to reinstate again something like a dormant, silent, real presence.'

A third category, and this will come as no surprise, was 'tired-ness'. Because at school I was often overtaken by an irresistible fatigue and, as was then said, 'my eyes clapped shut', I was finally sent to see a doctor. A form of 'sleeping sickness' was diagnosed and I was given medication. One morning, when I had bunked off school and had gone to the woods instead, I tumbled out of a tree. I had climbed up and then must have fallen asleep. I only woke up again in the back of an ambulance. That I suffered from such an extreme lack of attentiveness that it became a genuine concern was an ongoing topos of my childhood. A whole series of strange incidents offered proof of this. Once, while jumping down onto the threshing floor of my grandfather's barn, I jammed my knee into my eye. Four weeks of surgery and medical treatment followed, during which time I often thought of the biblical verse that urges one to guard something 'as the apple of your eye'. My mother had used the phrase often enough; with every new incident, my fear for my eyes grew. Despite this, I still managed to mislay the key to the apartment, my gym bag, my lunch box and so many of the objects of my childhood that were the apples of my eye and only much later did I recover them: as objects of poems.

Certainly, it is not possible wholly or even partially to identify the essence of writing with existential components such as absence or heaviness. There is a phrase Cees Nooteboom uses about the 'amalgam of fiction and reality' that makes up our true selves from the start.[5] Even so, perhaps it ought to be possible to gather up the various histories of the influences, the infirmities and the ingredients that, only later, become texts. It is these things that inform and shape our morphology, where the processes of distillation set to work and eventually create a poem.

If it is possible to view poems as what Joachim Sartorius calls 'nervous systems of the memory', then such a phrase conveys well what I have tried to do in several of my own texts. The factual, the concrete, only deserves its place in the text as a means of supplying atmosphere or providing the grounding for its delicate structure. This means that nothing ought to remain merely biographical in the narrow sense. It is never a question of 're-creation'. An early motif in my own experience suggests this: talk to things, converse with their substance. Objects are not important for their past reality, but as part of our perception, of hearing or seeing, of the very sensations they once helped to shape. They are the go-betweens and indirect paths taking you to the poem. Other things that help are the earlier-, the later-, the never-read canon 'flowing through the work' (Nooteboom again), the underlying craftmanship, and the gathering momentum from the painstaking, arduous work on the text. It is every single one of these things together that give rise to the complicated, labyrinthine mechanism out of which a poem emerges with its seemingly unsuspected, yet ultimately absolute necessity.

And yes, we do take it for granted that the writing of poems asserts itself with a degree of absoluteness. The motivation to write is not to be discovered in any advantageous configuration of our social lives, nor revealed in conversations about poetry, and is certainly not unearthed in lectures on poetics. Its real impetus precedes all of these and remains fundamentally invisible. Even in theoretical discussions and in questions to which poetic theory can give rise – whether among literary experts or between the poets themselves – the pre-poetic 'why' and 'whence' remains remarkably untouched.

'Everyone has only one song,' said the writer Paul Bowles in one of his last interviews.[6] (He was also a musician.) You recognise the song by its sound. The sound forms in the instrument we ourselves have become over time. Before every poem comes the story we have lived. The poem catches the sound of it. Rather than narrating the story, it narrates its sound. More than anything, 'Everyone has only one song' means that everyone *has* a song, and 'only one' means it's their *own* song. The search for it can take a long time. Years of eavesdropping on the melodies of others – good to listen in to, but is it your own particular song? You could say: the poem is something that, of necessity, asserts itself through the life of its author, it is his song, his faith in an 'absolute rhythm' that is his own personal rhythm. The belief is in an absolute sound that belongs to you alone. This strange excess, or 'intensity', which Ezra Pound's essay 'Vorticism' expressly focuses on in each of its brief statements, is what grounds the poem.

Writing poetry: a difficult way to live and, at the same time, the only possible way.

One aspect of all this is that the poem engages specifically with what cannot be verbalised. The mute and non-paraphrasable and its unique, existential origin: the particular qualities of any poem arise from these two subtly interwoven elements. The poem travels towards the unsayable, yet this is a movement without an end point. Perhaps this is why as soon as people start to reflect on the nature of poetry, there also begins a search for starting points, for the more or less definable beginning of a poem, a first handhold for comprehension. To this end, modernism has usefully brought to the discussion the notion of the body and its far-reaching involvement, its relationship with language and with the ineffable, with the essential. Tiredness, heaviness, absence – perhaps we mobilise our physiology when we speak or write. And yet we have already been written on. As we move through ourselves, we move through language.

When I think back to the dining table of my childhood, where we each sat, conscious of our own individual tiredness, I also remember there were occasions when we were less resigned to it. When my grandfather, Erich König (born 1908, died 1987), tried to resist his tiredness and the lethargy that followed it (accompanied by headaches and a dizziness we knew nothing of), when he tried to shake it off, it would take the form of an ill-tempered outburst. The meal itself would provide a ready trigger: even before he tasted it, he would yell something like 'too little salt', or 'too much salt', and he would shake his knife at my grandmother who always sat to his left at the table, the place nearest the stove. If the outburst continued, in other words, if he proved incapable of calming himself down, my grandfather would, there and then, announce he was going to kill himself. Out in the pigsty, he would find what he needed – the 'sow rope'. This whole business happened perhaps two or three times a year, most frequently at Christmas. On the first day of the holiday, it might be that my grandfather, to begin with, would smash my grandmother's present (on one occasion this was a beautiful, heavy desk, which he himself dragged with difficulty into the yard and chopped into kindling), and then – as he had declared – he would set about committing suicide. The tree he chose for the purpose was the oak tree that his own grandfather, Eduard (my great-great-grandfather, born in 1846, died in 1910), had planted as a Peace Oak at the end of the Franco-Prussian War in 1871. But either my grandfather had genuinely forgotten how inaccessibly high the lower branches of this huge, towering tree had grown, or he remembered well enough and expected his wife (whom he had just upbraided), with the help of the whole family, who were by now trailing along excitedly as if at a procession as he rushed to the sty, then from the sty to the tree, to persuade him (before he ever made it up the driveway to the oak) not to kill himself but rather to turn back to the house, the whole group of us, together again, now heading back to the disrupted meal table.

It is perhaps worth mentioning that this tree, the Peace Oak, occupies a prominent position in our family history. I think every generation developed its own special relationship with it or had some custom or tale associated with this huge tree beside the farm driveway. My mother tells me that, in his later years, my great-grandfather, Edwin König (born in 1876, died in 1964), used to tap the trunk of the oak – just where the trunk becomes the root and makes a little hump. He would tap it three times with his walking stick every time he passed. Why he did this remained a secret; he never revealed it, not even when pressed and not even to his favourite granddaughter (my mother, born in 1940), with whom he had a particularly close relationship. The fact is that Edwin König went to the village tavern every day at 4 p.m., passing the oak tree on his left, where he would tap the protrusion once, twice, three times. At exactly 6.30 p.m., he returned by the same route, again tapping the hump three times and then he was home.

I should ask your indulgence for this digression into the merely anecdotal: my real purpose here is to give an account of my writing by way of its origins and the associated states of perception (tiredness, heaviness and absence), to give you, so to speak, a poet's disposition from the ground up, as rooted in my birthplace . . . But now Edwin has intervened, he has knocked as it were, and he seems to be demanding his rights. A while ago, my uncle B, who, with great diligence and meticulousness, acts as keeper of the family history and has set up a family museum in the granary above the cowshed (previously the servants' quarters) and has filled it with items from the history of the farm and its line of patriarchs, going back through Eberhard, Erich, Edwin, Eduard König, and so on. The 'EK' of the family name had to be passed down to every generation: it was part of the farm property, printed in black on the sacks of grain and branded into the hides of the animals: 'EK'; the heir's Christian name had to begin with an 'E', that was fixed, long before his birth . . . So, my museum uncle, when he heard I was giving a so-called poetry lecture, handed over a small collection of poems with the observation that I ought not to presume that I was the *only one*: at any rate, he said, it is more than likely that it all started *from here*.

Until then, I confess, I had always assumed my family – at least every one of the verifiable generations – had consisted exclusively of farmers (and on the poorer, paternal side, of farm labourers) and, for the most part, this had seemed to be the case. But now, I held in my hands some poems written by my great-grandfather – the poems of Edwin König, the tapper of the oak hump and the last remaining undisturbed farmer in the fields around the town of Ronneburg.

To illustrate the kind of poetry my great-grandfather favoured, here are a few stanzas from a ballad to which he gave the title 'Hymn to Women':

[. . .]

Men would be masters of everything,
Would be crown of all creation!
Yet any capable of clear thinking
Knows women occupy that station.
Believe what I say, that every man
Must dance to the tune of women.
Women rule better than ever we can:
Wenches outdo we lads and men.

It's unattractive, the masculine face,
More like a file, prickly and rough!
Do men possess a delectable waist?
Quite the opposite, that's the truth!
Women have elegance and daintiness,
They have flounce and frill and ribbon.
So I say, how much more lovely she is:
Wenches outshine we lads and men.

'O the eternal feminine attracts,'
Says Father Goethe, so I've heard.
There is no man who manages that.
There's no reason to doubt his word.
O the eternal feminine attracts,
Like the magnetism of Hansen.
Nothing to be done to change the facts:
Wenches exceed we lads and men.

[. . .]

I will stop there and leave you with this excerpt from this eulogy, written around 1926. A footnote suggests singing these verses to the tune of the song 'A Free Life We Lead', a song of liberty by Friedrich Schiller, the melody of which dates back, in turn, to an eighteenth-century folk song. Goethe makes an appearance here too, and apart from the underlying feminist message, the reference to 'the magnetism of Hansen' is interesting. This is Carl Hansen, a world-famous hypnotist of the time, who convinced Sigmund Freud of the authenticity of hypnotic phenomena and, through his public demonstrations, sparked a veritable Hansen mania. Edwin König, this amusing, occasional poet, also feverishly rhymes his refrain 'lads and men' with someone who went by the name of 'Franzen' – well, my dear uncle, I would have to say, there really is an ancestor here, a poetic great-grandfather, and so there must surely be something in the genes, a poetical, genealogical bloodline (or whatever you might call it), at the very least here is an unacknowledged thread in the literary history of our East Thuringian region.

Yet the literary farmer of the period is actually not such an isolated case: Peter Huchel's grandfather, for example, also wrote ballads and satirical verses, and, at the turn of the century, news-papers and magazines were widely read on the large farms. Even my mother had piano lessons as a matter of course; field work and piano practice were not yet as far divorced from each other as we might nowadays assume. When I was a child, exploring the farm-house loft, I came across bound volumes of the magazine *At Home* (1904–1906). The subtitle of the periodical was 'A German Family Magazine' and it published novellas, poems and 'reviews of recent literature'; other sections also covered topics such as 'Historical', 'Military', 'Gardening' and 'Pictures of the Age'. Alongside this was a bound volume of the journal *Stage and World* which opened with a review of the 1902–1903 London theatre season. In these books (full of wonderful photographs of the theatre greats of the period, such as the 'peerless' Rosa Sucher, playing Eva in *The Mastersingers*, or the 'inimitable' Katharina Fleischer-Edel as the Countess in *The Marriage of Figaro*, etc.), I came across an invitation issued by the Literary Society of Altenburg, whose undersigned chair 'humbly takes the liberty' of inviting my great-grandfather and occasional poet Edwin König to a social gathering to be held in the banqueting hall of The Golden Plough.

The 'tired villages' – I should return to my theme. The tired villages – what a sweet-sounding description of the effects of continuous, low-dose radiation exposure. Of those who worked long term in the uranium mines, hardly any of them lived beyond the age of sixty-five. Following the forced evacuation of Culmitzsch and the razing of the village at the end of the 1960s, my grandfather, Gerhard Seiler, the man with the supernatural power when one of his hands was near the radio, was resettled in Teichwolframsdorf. He died there on 30 November 1981 suffering from 'Schneeberg lung disease'. This is what the illness, diagnosed in so many of the Wismut miners, and a direct consequence of radiation exposure, was called at the time. To this day, one hundred and fifty to two hundred cases of lung cancer (because that is what we are really talking about) are diagnosed every year because of radioactive exposure during the Wismut years.

The mining company, which has since then, in the post-reunification period, transformed itself into a redevelopment company, still retains the name Wismut, which originated under the Stalin-era government. In 2000, whole areas of the slag landscape formed part of the German World Expo and, in 2007, the German Garden Show laid topsoil over the wounded earth.

In April 2007, a few days prior to the opening of the Garden Show, I returned to the Thuringian landscape of my childhood, which by then was being referred to as the 'New Ronneburg

Landscape' – or so I read today in my notebook, number 42, in which I documented my return trip. The cone-shaped mountains of Ronneburg had gone. I stood on a hill at a point where mine shaft 381 had once descended and I gazed down into an artificially constructed valley. 'To ensure aftercare and a tourist experience, 16 km of commercial and hiking trails are being created,' I read on a noticeboard (and I made a note of it in my book).

The cherry trees were coming to the end of their flowering season and many of the other shrubs and flowers had yet to bloom. It had not rained for weeks. In some places, the 'New Landscape' in fact remained a barren brown, as if the body of the old, contaminated landscape was still lurking, as if the new skin had not yet fully grown to cover it.

Diagonally opposite me, on a geometrically laid-out incline (which, it was said, was supposed to echo slag heaps), the word WISMUT had been planted on the hillside in huge capital letters. I also came across two miniature pyramids, evidently representing the old cone-shaped heaps popularly referred to as the 'Pyramids of Ronneburg' or, by the miners, as the 'Ronneburg Tits'. In the middle of the valley there was a lookout tower which, on a nearby tourist display board, was designated an 'adventure tower'. Across the meadows, as if scattered by a generous hand, there were metal chairs, recliners and marquees. Though I liked the small wooden pavilion I found on the edge of the Kirschberg and though, without question, the redevelopment of the vast, gleaming uranium wasteland around Ronneburg was a blessing for the area, the fact that my childhood landscape had almost completely disappeared in the process made my heart break for a moment. This 'New Landscape' was no 'tourist experience' for me. My mother had been talking about our old 'wood field', as we called it, and I wanted to see if it was still there. The farm of her father, Erich König, son of Edwin König, the author of those occasional poems, included a stand of willow trees in a rather boggy hollow that must now be located close to the edge of the so-called 'New Landscape'. It was the most remote plot of land on the farm – three kilometres to the south, almost on the border between Thuringia and Saxony.

With map in hand, I followed a path a tractor had cut across the wheat field beyond the autobahn and I made for a patch of woods that I thought must be our old wood field. I thought of the child I had once been, who had run through the growing wheat in a pair of shorts and emerged on the far side with fiery red thighs that, for hours after, throbbed and pulsed. In fact, the old wood field now resembled an island of mixed woodland in the middle of the wheat fields – an island of birch, oak, fir, as well as willow. I found the willow stumps where the pollarding was still clearly visible. On the western horizon stood the Beerwalde uranium ore dump. I had arrived on the last island of my old childhood landscape, and in my mind I was already drafting something along these lines:

The wood field stands like an island in the wheat with a dry ditch encircling it. I feel perfectly happy here, alone; I talk aloud to myself. Viewed from the wood field, on the eastern horizon, looking towards Saxony, there stands the Beerwalde slag heap, an area that these days bears the half-intriguing, half-unsettling title of 'Aurora Resurrection', meaning something like 'Resurrection of the Dawn'. It is the Altenburger Land's project, their contribution to the Garden Show. At the summit, in the middle of the slag heap, they have created a so-called 'respected site', an area of thirty square metres where, it is said, nature is going to be left wholly to itself again – one of the Garden Show's ideals. A path leads to the top of the uranium dump, to this piece of 'liberated nature', and the route is marked by eleven cast-iron conical shapes whose base plinths carry philosophical inscriptions about respecting nature, including quotations from Albert Schweitzer, Friedrich Schleiermacher and even Joseph Beuys.

In the opposite direction, on the Thuringian horizon – in effect, directly out across the gently waving wheat fields – rises the spire of the church tower of my home village, Korbussen. To the left, the tall crown of our Peace Oak is just about visible – the oak of Eduard, Edwin and Erich, the oak of my great-great-grandfather, great-grandfather and grandfather, all long dead, and so, it is in this middle ground, located between my childhood garden and the Federal Garden, that I wander. It is here I 'rove' as we used to say, that rather soothing word with its ring of freedom: 'Well, do you want to head out for a bit longer, rove round a little?' or 'Where've you been off roving now?' or even 'You rover!' So I rove about the old wood field. I cross its island and, at the far end of it, I find the 'lay-up', as my mother always called it, there in a dip, the pond and, set between two birches, the seat. They would always take a break here, drinking barley coffee and eating pork dripping on bread with pickled gherkins . . . The seat has decayed and at one end the tree's expanding growth and it have grown together: the bark has closed round the plank's end like a mouth, holding it in the air.

For a while I squat down in front of the old seat. I look out across the field, at its rippling movements, its darker and lighter waves shifting as the wind blows, more or less strongly, lifting and flattening the wheat stalks. I watch how the light-dark patterns spread, how they sweep up towards the 'Aurora', to the Beerwalde slag heap that now lifts out of the ocean like a nearby reef.

At some point, for just a few moments, I probably dozed off. No surprise, because, without doubt, there I was at the heart of the tired territory, in one of its more magical spots. There was nothing but the rippling of the fields and me, grown tired in that old, familiar way, briefly losing consciousness. 'You, [. . .] whose existence makes me tired / like a cradle' as Rilke says in *The Notebook of Malte Laurids Brigge*. Then I had been dreaming perhaps, because I was suddenly roused by the roar of rutting rising up from the fields: two roebucks, circling each other threateningly and eventually heading off in the direction of the 'Aurora', accompanied by three does. I imagined the lead buck drawing the herd on, up along the philosophers' path, passing quotations from Joseph Beuys and Albert Schweitzer, climbing to the top of the uranium dump, up to the so-called 'respected site'. Up there, I heard the creature raise its bloodcurdling rutting cry – a tremendous, prolonged roaring from deep in its wild nature, a wake-up call, far and wide across the Garden Show, far and wide over the tired villages, over the places once known as Schmirchau, Lichtenberg, Gessen and Culmitzsch, now sunk in sleep under the rubble heaps, and over all those who had survived the vast uranium mines, a roaring without end that might at any moment smash the bell jar that had fallen over this region more than half a century ago . . .

We now understand that where, for hundreds of years, the Navajo of North America have been setting down their sacred images in sand, cornmeal and crushed flowers, uranium ore lay buried underground. The Sacred Land – where warnings of invisible dangers have been handed down through the generations – is radioactive. The largest underground uranium mine on earth is said to be on Mount Taylor, the sacred mountain of the Navajo.

In the Black Hills of South Dakota, places sacred to the Sioux are being destroyed by uranium mining. Generations of Native Americans, Navajo or Sioux, travelled across the land to find these particular places for the invocation of their spirits. The radioactive mineral was also buried beneath the fields around

Ronneburg – though we never had to search for the place, we already lived there. Why should the trance-like quality of such a region have affected us any less? One person makes a traditional sandpainting, another a poem.

(2001, revised 2020)

BABELSBERG:
BRIEF THOUGHTS ON ERNST MEISTER

Potsdam-Babelsberg is the name of the place where my then five-year-old daughter would go for ballet lessons. Twice a week, I took her there to the dance studio. The room where the girls practised classical ballet steps to the accompaniment of music had a large mirror at one end, beyond which there was a smaller, cramped room where their relatives – mostly mothers or grandmothers – sat on black chairs with green velvet cushions, anxiously watching the progress of their ballerinas. The mirror was see-through from that side. There, behind the mirror, with Tchaikovsky blaring from a cassette recorder and the dance teacher's instructions ringing in my ears, I balanced a book on my knees: its title was *Numbers and Figures* (*Zahlen und Figuren*), one of the volumes in the Rimbaud Press's Ernst Meister edition. In my notebook, dated 28 November 1996, it says, 'get hold of ernst meister' – though there is no indication where the idea had come from. Two months later, there I was, sitting behind the mirror, by turns reading and making notes, then glancing up to watch my daughter starting sequences over and over again, her first laborious steps in the art of dance, and then I would turn back to reading Ernst Meister's poem: 'It is the walking, the way / and nothing more'. This is the opening of *Numbers and Figures*, though for some reason, at that moment, I was dipping into the book from back to front. Towards the end of the book, I had read:

And within the circle,
the killing, yet siesta in the garden,
ice-skating elsewhere,
a common,
enduring, if not
homely
light, really
astonishing.

Or a little earlier in the volume: 'As for us, never at ease. / Too much is possessed by death.' Or: 'The unsyllabled / goodnight / of the world' and, still further back: 'A dead man / already forgotten / has wrapped himself in gold leaf' – my favourite lines from a poem which, as I have since discovered, Meister wrote after walking round a graveyard with Walter Höllerer. In these poems, published in 1958, death is already the leitmotif of Meister's work: 'Old crosses / and a new art.' And when I had worked my way back to the very beginning of the book, as I have said, I read: 'It is the walking, the way / and nothing more'. On the far side of the mirror, my daughter, incredibly, was practising a handstand, or, at the least, was bravely flinging her legs up into the air.

Walking and footsteps had been a theme in my own work around that time, and I had been gathering material on the subject. When I had added Meister's lines, I realised I already had a similar, almost identical passage on the subject of walking in my notes. It was something I had earlier taken from a poem by Nicolas Born in which he seemed, just a few years later, to be responding to Meister's poem: 'It is the walking – no headway'. Then I saw further correspondences between Meister's lines and some of the other phrases and images I had collected, such as between the deliberate bodily confusion in the 'First Epistle to the Corinthians' ('Now if the foot should say, because I am not a hand' etc.) and the confusions in Meister's first great book, *Exhibition* (*Ausstellung*): 'The man crosses his yellow legs as he sleeps. / Kneels his knees down into his mouth'. And while trying to imagine the fantastical walking of this poet from Hagen, his stride, his demeanour, I came across his author photograph at the front of the book, facing the title page. An old-fashioned portrait, I thought: studiedly posed, exaggerated in its seriousness, an almost Rilkean image of contemplation, yet not languid, or weak, but with all its energy focused on a point, beyond the picture, that remained invisible.

I looked at the image, the neat clothes, the pipe and tobacco tin on the table, the head propped on the hand: as an observer, you were not being invited into this picture. Rather it suggested a closed relationship between the author and whatever it was that remained unseen. It was a proud display that quite consciously – and not without a touch of pathos – gestured towards a wholly independent, autonomous meaning.

Nowadays writers smile in their author photographs, frequently they laugh, often heartily, revealing amazingly good teeth as if to say how comfortable and well-groomed life can be, even for a writer. If an author is not already grinning into the camera of his or her own volition, experienced photographers will soon ask if, perhaps, they couldn't look a little more friendly. Novice authors might want to present a face more appropriate to their text, or at least one that doesn't wholly undermine it. But then it is especially such inexperienced authors who will encounter a novice photographer, who immediately harangues them with: 'Give me a smile!' or 'How about a laugh?'

In contrast, Ernst Meister never laughs in the pictures which we designate as author photographs. In these portraits, the author represents his text. In these images, it is as in the poems: Meister keeps his life shut away, with an unconcealed seriousness and, something become increasingly rare in this context, a sense of what might be called dignity. These author images suggest what the poems have to say: 'This is mine.' In the case of Meister, this 'mine' is often interpreted as hermetic: as if any author were capable – as poetic debate often tends to suggest – of doing anything other than whatever is really his own. You might say: the poem – in being at one with the writer's life – is something that necessarily asserts itself, that it is the writer's own song.

(2003)

IN THE ANCHOR JAR

In writing, there are always those moments when you cannot make progress. Days when you pace round the room endlessly, around the material, when in actual fact you are circling yourself, repeatedly mouthing something aloud, to your ear, only to hear the same thing over and over again: it's not right. A dervish squats on the voice and constricts it. For as long as it takes, until the utterance is right, then he grows animated, he adds his part, that ineffable something to the whole, and on both sides the feeling of gratitude is great. As great as the despair when things are not working out.

One evening, about eight years ago, when I had been similarly stymied for a while and was close to despair, I took myself down to the cellar. It may have been that I was already a bit disoriented, at any rate exhausted, like a creature that has spent too long circling an invisible prey. I explored the shelves in the semi-darkness and eventually found what I was looking for: a few empty glass jars covered in coal dust. When I had washed them off, I could see the maritime symbol they carried on the lid and the lettering of an old, comforting name: they were ANCHOR jars. Ribbed glass jars made by the Anchor company in Saxony – jars that had been used and handed down in my family for several generations. Back at my desk, I took a pair of scissors and, without a moment's hesitation, carefully started to cut up my drafts. I cut right through verses and stanzas, seldom leaving many lines together, scissoring words or groups of words from the page. And it felt good, satisfying, productive, so I also cut up earlier manuscripts and papers that had been languishing in a drawer and I filled my Anchor jars with them. Then I sealed them up. I attached a length of adhesive tape as a label and dated the jars with the year and the season: *Autumn 1996*. I had preserved them.

At the time, I did not feel the least inclination to account for such a bizarre action. That only changed when I broke open my jars in the summer of 2003 and I had to ask myself: why had writing turned to preserving that evening? Why this rather helpless resort to an old, unliterary process?

Making preserves: every year there was a fruit harvest that got completely out of hand. For days on end, over-supply and stockpiling round the hearth in the steam-filled utility kitchen and, in front of it, the hurriedly gathered outlines of several familiar shapes. On the big burners stood the preserving pans, which, with thermometers protruding from their lids like antennae, looked like nothing so much as spaceships ready to launch. From my vantage point at the kitchen table, my command centre, I viewed these ships' failure to achieve lift-off with a critical eye. It seemed perfectly possible they might explode at any moment. In what was called a 'good year' there was a deluge from the garden that quite swamped us. I can still hear, 'There's too much,' or 'I can't manage this,' then a groaning from the vaulted cellar, where the filled jars were being stacked, no longer just on shelves, but along passageways and on the stone steps that led directly into the cellar from the kitchen. From the start, it seemed inconceivable that all this produce would ever be consumed. But to give up, to abandon something to decay, that was simply out of the question. On the contrary, additional jars, rubber bands and clips were hastily procured and at long last, several days later, the invasion had finally been contained and despatched into the Anchor jars of that particular vintage, examples of which, simply due to the sheer numbers, would still be turning up in the backs of cupboards decades later, the fruit covered with a thin, chalky crust that was claimed not to be mould and so no reason not to consume it. What I really felt about this I only came across later in the cellar poem, 'Down There', by W. H. Auden: 'Encrust with years of clammy grime, the lair, maybe, / Of creepy-crawlies or a ghost'.

It was only in the context of her war experiences, the anxieties associated with them, that I could make much sense of my grand-mother's talk after this onslaught – and even in her exhaustion – of 'the blessing of fruit that keeps on giving'. No – no such corre-sponding hardship had been the precursor to my writing crisis. And no, I did not consider my scribblings as 'giving', quite the contrary. Yet, even in the midst of my distress, I had impulsively turned to just this practice, from my own upbringing, with which a seemingly impossible circumstance might be managed via a mechanical process. And why should I not think of my jars as part of the storehouse of technical aids about which Edgar Allan Poe writes in his *Philosophy of Composition*? With the help of these jars, I had not merely set my material aside, I had transposed it in time.

A preserve retains juice and hence freshness, yet everyone knows preserves do not taste like the original fruit. Between the fruit and the jar that is later opened comes the method, the process and – above all – time. The preserved fruit tastes of time. Today I would say that the best thing about a poem when you recite it to yourself is that it tastes of time. Working on the poem amounts to an investment of time, in the proper sense of the word. The result is the poem's temporal power, which in turn is essential for the potency of its imagery. It is not a question of any specific verb tense: its fascination is with the passage of time. In my work on a poem, for example, this means delving into the past for the very moment, for the first stirrings of the poem, the moment of its inception. Working with this particular, non-paraphrasable moment is difficult: on the one hand, it must be preserved and, if I succeed in doing this, it will emerge, intact, in the final version as a kind of infant form of the poem. Despite all the painstaking and tiresome labour, it is precisely from this that the completed poem will draw an essential part of its power. The other requirement, as I have said, is the vertical work, revealing the layers of time within which this poem's core is embedded, the search for the lines of its magnetic field across history, biography or technology.

Today, when I think back to the sense of pleasure that I experienced in cutting up my manuscripts, I understand things more clearly. Apart from the satisfaction that the aggressive, purely destructive aspects of this action might have yielded, there must have been a vague expectation, in the depths of my despair, that what I was doing would not only liberate the present, but also create the future. I was transposing my material into an 'ideal now' in the future, a forthcoming present of wonderful writing moments that would be elicited by this material when I could re-encounter it as if new – moments of awakening, of grasping before understanding, which the poem needs in order to be a poem: in those jars lay dreams of my future writing.

Anchor jars – in some ways they seem the opposite of a message in a bottle. In 1958, on receiving the Bremen Literature Prize, Paul Celan described the poem as a message in a bottle. An Anchor jar and a message in a bottle: both are receptacles with a maritime association, yet their movements, their locations, their histories are quite different. In the case of the message in a bottle, there is a forsakenness, a sense of something having been lost on both sides, both sender and recipient are afflicted by it.

Doubts about the addressee, even about the legitimacy of contemplating an addressee, and the hope – more or less besieged by these doubts – for some specific impact resulting from the poem and its language: nowadays, it seems to me, these ideas have been absorbed into the act of writing itself, they have become an element of the self-reflection involved in the process of writing. Doubt: the author no longer needs to propose it, there is hardly any reason for him to address this difficult subject in any extra-literary way. When I write today, from the outset I can no longer assume the role of a self-evident speaker of a message destined for an audience. This is a definitive shift in the author's disposition that has an impact not only on his methods but also on the text he writes. A message in a bottle and an Anchor jar – instead of speaking in vague terms about the 'author', perhaps I would do better to focus on the receptacles, because it is only at first sight that the differences between them predominate. With both these vessels, time is gained, time is invested. The Anchor jar, with its fragments, can then perhaps be viewed as an experiment in the deferral of the promise implied in the image of a message in a bottle on its way. Or to put it another way: as a message in a bottle, these Anchor jars were *en route* into my own writing. Both these vessels serve to transform the failures of the present, by way of an old technology, into a hope for the future. And in this way, the present becomes more manageable, and the work can also proceed as, eventually, it did in my own case.

In cutting up and preserving my manuscripts (without boiling them, of course) there certainly lay my wishful thinking to return language to the status of matter, a poetic raw material, treating it, if such a thing is possible, as a kind of natural substance. At first glance, my picking up the scissors might look brutal, but I only severed structure and I did not harm a single word in the process. Today I see the whole procedure more as an act of conservation, of precaution, also in the sense of laying up stores. Yet the process of preserving does not only represent a desire for conservation and a wish to return language to substance, it also represents the wish to seek out the particular place where it may be properly accommodated.

As a child, every day after school my job was to light the stove. Stove-ash-bucket-cellar-coal-stove: that was the orbit of those afternoons. It might take me an hour to re-emerge from the cellar. There was a numbingly sweet dead-mouse smell in the air and a bluish gleam of cyanide in the corners. The cellar sent me into dream states, states of ease and complete absence. Almost motionless, I stood with a candle in my hand (the electric light was broken) and cast its light over the shelves, or better to say I eavesdropped on them. Behind me on the wall hung the huge baseboard of a model railway, beside me my great-grandmother's old armoire, but before me were arrayed rows of preserves, a collection of museum proportions. Reading the jars, I made out the neatly inscribed adhesive tape, my mother's handwriting, or my grandmother's, occasionally an unfamiliar hand with dates that, to my childish imagination, referred to an inconceivably distant past. Perhaps this was my first reading in the passage of time. There was a silence that seemed to emanate from those dusty jars and to which I responded with a kind of muttering, something vocalised, a conversation with myself. A kind of primal scene, perhaps, in the story of one's own voice. The mute presence of these preserves, their organic immobility, stirred something in me, stirred me to inchoate sounds. At least it did until I reached the lower shelves with my candlelight, my reading light. There sat the jars containing meat and sausage, the archives of liver, blood and fat. Every year, on my grandfather's farm, we still slaughtered our own livestock. The slaughter party meant: the child gripping the drumming limbs of the staked, panicking animal as the butcher applied the bolt gun to its head. Or: the child being asked to come hold the animal's intestines while they are rinsed over the sink, the child vomiting. He gets poured his first vodka, which he flings behind him, against the laundry-room wall. So, there are things to smile about and, by way of consolation, one half of the much-coveted brain, which is said to have miraculous powers, and its little oily mass is already sizzling in the pan. Every year a slaughter day, every year new jars of black pudding, liver sausage, minced meat – for my entire childhood and youth, this is what filled my sandwiches. Home-butchered meats were precious and highly prized, but my problem with them was the lack of variety – though nothing as bad as Woyzeck's bean diet, of course. If you are what you eat, as we used to say, if I believed in this morphological short circuitry, then every time I went to fetch the coal, did I not have to fight off the thought, standing in front of those shelves, that I was staring into my own future, indeed catching a glimpse of myself in those jars? Driven by my writing crisis, I had clearly been determined to overcome the considerable levels of physical disgust that contemplating such preserves tended to produce in me. To see myself, not only provisioned with these jars, but also prepared, in the true sense of the word, I mean, to find myself in what was yet to come, that remained the crucial experience.

Everything is connected: an understanding of passing through time and of the power of time in the poem. A message in a bottle, an Anchor jar – vessels for the extraction of time. The desire for a substance-like state of language and, eventually, a place for its accommodation, its contemplation, ultimately a place for the creation of the poem, grounded, hushed, filled with absence. And when I look through my notebooks of this period, it becomes clear that my obsession with preserving as a literary technique went hand in hand with the discovery of material from my childhood, that is, the actual time of such preserving, of archiving moments that later appear timeless in the poem. In this sense, the point at which I got blocked on that particular occasion, and at which I turned to scissors and cutting, marked a moment of change, a reorientation in my own writing.

So, at last, back to the jars. There were times when I picked them up and shook them; I could make out individual words through the ribbed glass. But mostly the jars just stood alongside note-books; more recently they were hidden behind books on a shelf. Something happened over time. My writing had finally moved on and the promise that was preserved in those jars, or that I had taken to be in them, now seemed dubious. Sure, I had thought about it on occasions, but I had always refrained from opening the jars. Imperceptibly, their meaning had changed before my eyes. I had to admit to myself that now, instead of a promise, I sensed a kind of threat: vessels in which nothing more nor less than an old writing crisis had been preserved. Something to be kept locked away at all costs; at best, to be thought of as a symbol of coping with it. But as so often happens, curiosity and recklessness won the day and, seven years later, I opened the jars, though I first took the precaution of packing their contents, sight unseen, into several envelopes and stowing them in my luggage on my way to Los Angeles, where I was to spend the summer. To be honest, the outcome was oddly sobering. Beside a window that looked out across Santa Monica Bay, among the scattered bits of paper on my desk, there was, with hardly any exceptions, nothing that had been forgotten. Over the course of the previous few years, almost every word, every connection, had been incorporated, in one way or another, into my poems. I had preserved; I had set aside, yet nothing had been lost to the writing, nothing had been lacking, nothing but time. In the Anchor jars, everything had taken its time: the words had taken their time till *their* text had emerged and I too had taken the time to find a belief in myself and in this voice.

(2004)

SUNDAYS I THOUGHT OF GOD

Sundays I thought of god as we
travelled around town on the bus.
at the roadside by the fire pond stood

an electricity substation and out of the air
three and forty cables converged on this
house of hard-baked brick; there

in the substation at the roadside lived god. I saw
how he sat in his nest of cables
hunkered down shut in by brick walls

with no window on the ground there
in the dark at the roadside behind
a door made of steel

sat the good lord; he was
infinitely small & laughing
      or asleep[7]

I wrote this poem six or seven years ago and I have not thought much about it since. Yet, on those occasions when I have read it aloud, it has often seemed to me as if, one day, it might open a way to something, as if I might be able to pass through that door by the roadside and enter a narrative space. The perceived connection between God and electrical voltage was bound up with the sustained, humming noise that, as a child, it was impossible for you to ignore. That high voltage drone that could be either inside or outside your own head. It was a sound that set off flights of fancy, given wing by the little sign with a skull-and-crossbones and the words: *Danger to life! No entry by order of police. Parents are responsible for their children.* In front of that door, more than once in my imagination, I'd had visions of myself visiting my parents in prison. And then I was sorry for everything I had done, for my now all-too-obvious ingratitude, although above all I felt sorry for myself. Now, I was in effect an orphan and a state children's home awaited me. Perhaps I might be allowed to spend one more night in my own room? But what should I take with me? And when would they come to get me? In my mind, I wept and yet – wicked and guilty as I was genuinely feeling, as conscious as I was of my own irresponsibility – somewhere on the edge of that imagined grief, I could not dismiss the desire to violate the prohibition. I stood paralysed for a few moments, paralysed by the desire to transgress. Then again, how calm and clear-sighted one becomes in the face of prohibition: flushed with the possibilities that transgression promises.

There was a magic in such places. Flowing through each of these cables, there might run a story that, if I wanted, I simply had to listen to. All I had to do was to get closer to the transformer, perhaps put my ear to its heavy steel door, something that, even in my fear, I felt I was prepared to do.

2.

The fear had been nurtured by the one-armed instructor who, from Class 5 onwards, taught us technical education. Fear of electricity: the instructor explained how even the smallest of electrical shocks was likely to lead to a cardiac arrest. The central figures in his tales of disaster were mostly children of our age, whose recklessness and spitefulness spoke volumes. They had murdered classmates with their antics. There seemed to be an endless catalogue of these incidents. Almost every lesson began with the story of an accident, that is, with a group of quite thoughtless, despicable students and their soon-to-be-dead companion. The instructor: he wore thick glasses and a brown nylon smock. The end of his right sleeve was folded neatly and flatly into a side pocket and, just to be on the safe side, fastened there with a clip.

For the duration of each of his stories, I stared at the empty sleeve. I would try to tear my gaze away, but my eyes snagged on it. With the reiteration of these stories, I became convinced that the instructor's arm itself had fallen foul of an assault involving electricity and (though this was quite impossible) that the perpetrators were present among our ranks, hiding, cowardly, ducking down behind the students in front of them. With both hands, they would be clinging to the shelf under their bench so as not to leap up suddenly, in the middle of the story, falling to their knees in the middle aisle of the classroom, yelling, absurdly, in front of everybody, 'It was me, it was me . . .'

As work went on in those lessons, sawing or filing at the bench vices, the instructor would come close to us and we wanted at all costs to avoid any contact with his empty sleeve. It was as if there might still be a wound hidden there, still painful, or one that might rupture if we were not careful. The instructor was not to be touched. And he was often irritable, surly and very strict with us. His manner inculcated fear, perhaps even more than his appearance. Of course, the fact that he was missing an arm would cause him endless difficulties. There were complicated situations when he needed to demonstrate something to the class. Beneath the classroom window, there was a workbench on which a number of small vices were mounted. During a demonstration, one of these vices had to serve in place of the missing hand. If a piece of work slipped out of the vice, not one of the students dared to come forwards to pick it up off the floor. Motionless, we maintained our obedient semicircle round the man and the vice, no one even thinking of stepping up to help. Such an action would have violated the prevailing air of constrained awe too obviously and, we felt, it would have been tantamount to an admission of guilt. And who knew what might happen then?

3.

As and when the occasion arises, it is possible to pick up the thread of a narrative from any point. To stay with the electrical image: from any consumer, from any plug socket, I can reach the substation. Everything is part of the subject, whether you call it *electricity* or *God*. Everything is connected and involved in the story. Before you get caught up (all too soon) in the to and fro of the tale, you catch a glimpse of the distribution network, the consumption, the various sources with their competing tariffs, you hear the triple-phase meter in the cellar, under the stairs you descend for the first time, each time, to gain entry to the story – before your eyes, you see the whole network of silent electricity consumers.

A poem, on the other hand, often begins by turning aside from the centre of action, even if it is initially only towards a sequence of sounds or a particular rhythm. Compared to a story, it induces its material differently. Even so, it can be a narrative. After reading or listening to such a poem, you feel you have been told something, but you are simply not able to say clearly what it was, because it was so many things at once. The resonance chamber of a poem should not be smaller than that of a novel. Any good poem, therefore, could provide the metaphorical, rhythmical or gestural kernel of a novel. The narrative gesture establishes the poem's connection to the origin of the genre, to the epic and its singers, a connection that to this day has not really been renewed. At the end of his Harvard lecture on narrative, which includes a critique of the modern novel, Jorge Luis Borges says: 'I believe that the poet will once again become a maker. By that, I mean he will tell a story and he will also sing it. And we will no longer consider these two things distinct, even as we do not think they are distinct in Homer or Virgil.'

4.

We must not forget that the object is the best messenger from a world above that of nature: there is, in the object, at once a perfection and an absence of origin, something closed and something shining, a transformation of life into matter (matter is more magical than life) and finally: a silence that belongs to the realm of the miraculous.

(Roland Barthes, 'The New Citroën', *Mythologies*)

According to the poem quoted at the beginning of this essay, God 'was laughing / or asleep'. It is Sunday and God is at rest among his cable ends. We ourselves seldom rested on a Sunday. True, we did not go to church either, but every Sunday for years my father and I would walk past the church on our way to the garage. Often the bells would be ringing as we made our way down the hill, only to turn off just before the churchyard wall and then we would follow a narrow, cobbled way lined by an avenue of chestnuts down into the Elster Valley. In the valley, beside the railway embankment, stood the row of garages.

To begin with, our work in the garage was nothing other than practical. Under my father's guidance, I demonstrated that I was capable of understanding and repairing a machine myself. My father worked on his Russian car, a Zhiguli, while I worked on my Simson SR1. This was my first motorbike, really a moped, really barely more than a bicycle with an auxiliary motor. I had found it on my grandparents' farm, but it would not start. So I pushed it to the top of a pile of sand between the barn and the farm garage and let myself roll back down with as much volume of self-generated engine noise as I could muster, over and over again, until I was exhausted. In fact, the prosody of my engine, powered by the imagination, owed more to a large-bore BMW engine and little to the narrow-bore, single-cylinder moped engine, the actual sound of which – a high-pitched yowling yet bee-like sound (yes, yowling bees) – I had no inkling of as yet.

Incidentally, I never caught sight of any genuine churchgoers on our walks to the garage. Perhaps the ringing was just a habit, nine o'clock every Sunday, or perhaps the bells in the tower were run off some kind of timer circuit. If so, they rang out automatically and there was no need for anybody to attend church on the day at all. But thanks to the absolute regularity of our own Sunday routines – from getting up for breakfast to leaving the house – our walk always seemed to be given a blessing: with the ringing of the bells, the air seemed fresher, as if purified, and our feet trod more steadily down the hill, often accidentally falling into a lockstep that did not particularly trouble us.

How we appeared: my father in his blue overalls with a baseball cap (then we called it a peaked cap) and me in a ludicrous grey knee-length smock with a company logo ironed onto the breast pocket, ugly, already peeling off, coming away at the corners. The smock was my work gear for the 'Lessons in Technical Production' which, from Class 7 on, we attended in the so-called 'shovel sheds'. For a few hours a week, shrouded in toxic fumes, we would be permitted to immerse ourselves in the secrets of socialist manufacturing in an actual 'export factory', i.e. a factory of 'vital importance'. For a long time afterwards, I thought the folding shovel – much like the folding camp bed and the folding bicycle – was a specifically East German invention. The folding shovels manufactured in the shovel sheds were despatched to our National People's Army. And, with a different finish, in part consisting of the application of special labels, they were also exported to Western Europe, allegedly even going to supply NATO.

Around this time, I became obsessed with a particular image: that, with the advent of the third world war (which we all knew to be imminent *at any moment*), armed forces carrying shovels from our factory would come face to face with each other. As we drilled the holes in the handles, threaded the screws, or painted the steel parts (coughing in the fumes), I found myself imagining that critical moment. Either the soldier has a strap on his assault pack to attach the shovel or, when it is folded, he secures it over his belt like a peg. He needs a shovel to be able to dig in, at lightning speed, depending on combat conditions, either finding cover in an open field or at the edge of a wood. And, if required, our well-forged and neatly painted shovel, with its somewhat sharpened blade, could of course also be used in close combat as a cutting or stabbing weapon, at least once it had been unfolded. I imagined two soldiers, lost between the lines, tangling together in hand-to-hand combat as in the opening of the Charlie Chaplin film *The Great Dictator*. But suddenly they pause, standing face to face amidst the gun smoke, the shells booming round them and, because their uniforms have been rendered unrecognisable by their wrestling in the mud, they suddenly see each other as allies, primarily because of the shovel each of them has in his grasp. And, of course, they are quite mistaken, realising this almost immediately (after all the paintwork on the shovels differs), yet they do not start over with the stabbing and shooting but rather talk shop: yes, the folding mechanism of the shovel is not really very effective, the union nut works loose too easily if you are digging or cutting, so the shovel is liable – in the heat of the moment – to collapse suddenly, resulting in painfully bruised fingers. And one of the men holds his hand up to the other as proof.

Perhaps it was because of the church bells, or because of our walking in lockstep, that such things went through my mind on our way to the garage. Then, suddenly, we were standing at the garage door which you opened by lifting it up overhead. With a pleasant, dark, rolling sound, it slid away on well-greased rails. In the long row of these pivoting garage doors, ours had recently become the only lime-green one, so that now, when I came alone, I no longer needed to count along to find its location. There had been plenty of paint left over after painting my SR1, so my father, using the air compressor, had carried on and used it on the door. At that time, there was a collective understanding of how a row of modern garages, built from hollow reinforced-concrete panels with pivoting doors, ought to look. There was an aesthetic accord among the garage members that set itself in opposition to the so-called colourful 1970s. So, with this lime green door, my father had said a definite goodbye to the *garage association*, as it was called. And I suffered because of this – in the way that every child of a certain age is embarrassed if his parents break with convention. Of course, it doesn't take long before the reverse is true. The association held regular meetings, run by the chair (Polski Fiat, two doors to our right) and a deputy who collected the rent (Zaporozhets, later Skoda, somewhere to our left). It was a group whose solidarity was founded on the shared labour of building the garages in the first place and reaffirmed when every one of them was flooded by the nearby White Elster in 1982.

The windowless depths of the garage opened before us. Lights were switched on and we each took down our toolbox from the shelf. We began with jobs that, early on, we still gave an account of: we named and explained things to each other, their 'remedial' effects, their preventive purpose, their monetary value. These were lessons; my father's voice, the long pauses between phrases, his approval when I was able to explain why I was doing any particular job. I would explain why I wanted to take this or that thing apart, to clean it, oil it, preserve it with rust inhibitor, all those things that I had previously heard him say and now I was happily repeating. I was at the right age, not yet too rebellious, and though my enthusiasm for technology, my emotional investment in the settings of the carburettor or the ignition, had its limits, I could enjoy this form of calm and attentive activity, these quiet routines reinforced by repetition. On these Sundays, in this, if not secret, then at least remote place, something was being passed from one to another, something that had nothing to do with science or technology.

Soon the reciprocal explanations of our actions grew less frequent. If we spoke at all, our voices soon drifted away from the concrete action; they remained in the space, but only as a sort of ambient backdrop to the movements of mouth and hand. What was left was a form of devotional activity. What was being spoken was not important. The incantation only required some tools, something to unscrew, something to take apart and reassemble again. Specific words and phrases would hover briefly in the air, artfully scattered grace notes in the quiet, like 'come on', or 'dammit', or 'there you go'.

So it was, together but lost in our own thoughts, that we made our way down to the garage, a walk which — when I was not concerned about my embarrassing smock and hoping none of my friends would spot me (though, as a rule, there was no one about anyway) – had become a real pleasure. The fresh morning air, the quick pace, the chestnut trees. And so it was with a wonderfully clear head that I stood in front of my machine – my father standing before his – and quietly we began our ritual.

Everything starts with the laying out of rags for the tools or the engine parts. After this prologue, various things might follow: disassembling the carburettor, adjusting the ignition, cleaning the exhaust, bleeding the brakes (I help my father with this), simple tasks as well as more difficult ones. And questions keep arising: is the carburettor needle in the right position? Should it be a notch higher or lower? So, try it out, give it a test drive; the old position was the correct one. Or adjusting the ignition: I need specific tools. I need to read up in the owner's manual on ignition timing, the ignition timer, and so on. There are some tasks I am not in the mood for every Sunday. I favour the simple jobs. I kneel on an old blanket in front of my engine and clean the electrodes of an unscrewed spark plug with a small wire brush. I clean long and hard, every now and then the little brush accidentally scraping across my fingertips, and, though this ought to hurt, I hardly notice it. I am in a state of devotion. As I kneel on my blanket, my back slightly bent, my gaze drifts off between the cylinder head and the petrol tank into the air. I am relaxed, and these days I would say that in such a moment I was becoming conscious of my own existence and, at the same time, of the existence of something other, something beyond me which remained invisible to the eye. Shortly after twelve o'clock, the tools are cleaned and packed away and by twelve-thirty we are back home in time for lunch.

For a while, this is how it was every Sunday. Later, I could not stand the garage anymore. I was seventeen or eighteen and felt too old for that kind of devotion. All I wanted to do now was to ride, not maintain, and certainly I had no time for metaphysics. I remember the day I saw my last motorbike for the last time, an MZ TS 250/1. It was in the backyard of a condemned house in Leipzig where I had parked it during the confusion in the months after the Wall came down. I had been having a few issues with the ignition, probably just some minor fault that caused the plugs to oil up after a few kilometres, but which repeatedly caused the engine to flood. I could not be bothered to fix it. I had to move on. I told myself I would take care of it in a few days' time. When I went back, almost a year later, the house was deserted, the yard piled with rubbish and there, in the middle of it all, was *my motorbike* – no petrol tank, no headlight, it had been completely cannibalised. First, I used a stone to break off the little plate, riveted to the frame, which carried the model type and the vehicle number. Then – I was already in tears – I hammered away at the number stamped into the bike's steel frame until it was completely illegible.

What I still have today: the electrode brush, the ignition clock, *all my tools*, carried in a toolbox through the years. The box is in the shed next to the house. I can go there and pick something out, such as the feeler gauge. Its various feelers are like 'tongues', twenty tongues that fold out and range in thickness from 0.1 to 2 millimetres. The 0.4 millimetre tongue, for example, was used to set the gap between the anode and cathode of the motorbike spark plugs. The gap was right if the tongue could be inserted between the electrodes; it was optimal if it stuck a little. Today, when I have this feeler gauge in my hand, when its still slightly oily tongues slide out of the retaining case in the shape of a fan as if by themselves, when I touch the metal, when I open and close the fan, it occasionally happens that I find my way back to the old state of devotion. When I fold it up again, when the little tongues slip into the steel case and are pressed one to the other, there is a soft scrunching sound, a wonderful sound, almost like a language, a thrill: so, I unfold the fan again, then fold it back once more, but more slowly this time, moving each tongue separately, very slowly, and each one scrunches differently, softly, out, then in. Sure, it is a weird picture: as if transfixed, somebody is standing in a shed, in front of his toolbox, and he is folding a feeler gauge open, then shut. The feeler gauge belongs to the inventory of sacred things, to a time when the garage was a kind of church.

5.

The poem 'Sundays I thought of God' also reminds me of my Sunday job as a barman and of the day when I saw the man on the hydraulic lift.

Between 1991 and 1994, I worked in a basement bar on Oranienburger Strasse in the Mitte district of Berlin. It was a cellar converted by the residents of the building – no creature comforts, cheap prices for beer and tinned food, and called the Assel, meaning 'Woodlouse'. The Assel was the first of its kind, though it was very quickly followed by similar places, as well as Italian and Mexican restaurants and, closer to the synagogue, several Jewish shops. On Sundays, there were already quite a few tourists visiting during the daytime. In the evening, the prostitutes appeared and then the street belonged to them. When they took a break, or just needed to seek out some warmth, they congregated, drinking cocoa, at a round table right next to the bar where we served. In fact, the table had established itself over the years as the staff table, but the women ignored that, or were not even aware of it, and none of us would have dared to point it out. They were welcome. Their presence drew other visitors into the bar and they always tipped well.

One quiet, early Sunday evening, there was a sudden commotion outside. One of the women was shouting something down to the bar from halfway up the stairs and everybody hurried out. At the end of the street, just a hundred metres away, on the trams' turning loop, lots of people had gathered. As I got nearer, I saw tourists, passers-by, prostitutes and their clients, all of them forming a kind of circle, strangely quiet and standing at a noticeable distance, as if behind a line drawn by a pair of compasses. In the middle of this circle was a hydraulic platform which had been extended up into the air to reach the tram's overhead cables. Everybody was looking up.

Because, in setting all this down here, I have the sensation now of drawing closer once again to what was then happening, I want to carry on, but to give an account of it using the exact wording of the first pencil notes I made in the moment, or just after the moment, a kind of first rough draft that I will reproduce here without changing anything, either phrasing or syntax:

The story is about a man on a cherry picker. This morning, in the bathroom, I had to think about the man who had raised his platform into the tram's overhead power cables. To start with, the following is what must have happened: when the lift accidentally came into contact with the high-voltage lines, the man was knocked down, the man fell down into the tub, he keeled over into the basket, the enclosed space at the top. Now he was gone. I saw for myself what happened next. The man was gone. But you could hear him kicking, writhing, his body striking the tub & quietly, like a little campfire, something was crackling, his body, you could hear the electricity, you could hear the voltage, then it all went quiet. When the platform no longer swayed and so lost contact with the overhead power lines – perhaps by no more than a few millimetres – first of all you saw the man, or something that resembled the head of a man, slowly, uncertainly and as if very wearily inching up over the edge of it, over the edge of the raised platform & then a hand: there's no doubt, the man in the tub was trying to get up, there's no doubt his whole effort was focused on groping towards the button of this, his self-operated mechanism, so that he might be able to lower the platform back to the ground, back to earth. But the man was weighed down already, he was grey from the juice of the overhead lines and his upper body teetered (a lot) (trembled) & like the hands, his hands (already) (shrivelled hands) flapped backwards & forwards on the edge of the lift tub like ill-tempered birds (grey-tempered). This caused / so that the whole raised platform began to sway again, and again the little campfire crackled, and the grey plasticine, his kneaded head, with a (agonisingly formed) cry, toppled backwards into the orange tub. Now you could make out, as before, the scraping and thumping of his body against the metal, then it again grew quiet. Below him too, where we were all standing until, once more, his grey hands, the birds, hopping again, but more slowly . . . I

Here the notes break off. Up on the swaying platform, the catastrophe played itself out. I remember the same sequence repeating itself several times. Even today, when I try to get a grip on the event, it is the small details that surface. But to begin with, there was utter horror, something was taking place, suddenly, out of nowhere, something happens. Above all, there were those sounds, the man's scrabbling in the basket, his futile efforts to tear himself away from his misfortune. Worst of all: his moaning and whimpering, his pleading without speech, nothing but noises. That is something not mentioned in my original notes. I was not able to render it (and I still cannot), yet it is something that has stayed with me, in my memory, all the more vividly: his long-drawn-out, pleading *Auuuu auu auu* like a little child crying, crying out his unhappiness, but in a man's voice.

The first, immediate sense of shock was followed by a second: why did no one come to help? Where were this man's co-workers, his team, where was the fire brigade, the ambulance – there were no emergency services of any kind (they had certainly been called, repeatedly), no help arrived. The belief that, in an emergency, someone is there to offer help in a professional, highly organised way, even, if needed, to rescue us: is that not one of the promises of this urban society in which, at least in this way, we feel ourselves so embedded? But here, there was only the utter horror of what suddenly happened and the horror that followed: nobody came to help. The modern world had failed to function when the man on the lift had an accident. The high voltage flowing through the platform isolated the man – no one would have dared to approach. The event had become untouchable in the most literal sense. But then, as this sense of helplessness began to be felt more generally, we also felt, as spectators, increasingly stricken by it and hence progressively more disconnected from our environment. Or did our assumptions about that environment simply no longer apply? Had we actually been mistaken about it and only now, confronting this accident, were we coming to see the truth of it? Or to put it another way, the whole incident seemed to suffer a loss of connection: to this busy street, to this city and its society, and it was not only the man on the platform, but we too, with him, standing, bearing witness to his tragedy, partaking as spectators as it unfolded, we too felt abandoned, yet enveloped. The sense of utter helplessness grew, and it took both the man and us into its arms.

I do not know how to describe this more clearly: the next thing, perhaps, was a sense of rapture, of being entranced. Above our heads, the man was still crackling in his tub, whimpering his childlike cries, trying to stand up, his hands, his head and the swaying of the platform . . . And, for the first time since child-hood, I seriously thought about praying. Not only for the man in the tub: I need to be clear about this, for the sake of accuracy . . . I would say 'in all honesty' were it not for the impression of patting myself self-righteously on the back. Catastrophe was unmistakably and unremittingly present; there was no one to shield us from it. There was no mitigating response to the sudden calamity, to death. Now, alongside my sense of compassion, there was a sense of being forsaken, a feeling that involved me as well as the man on his platform.

I thought of Kafka's short story, 'Conversation with the Supplicant', in which a man says his misfortune is a teetering misfortune ready to fall upon anyone who touched it. The sup-plicant lives from other people's observing him as he prays, and the man on the lift died while we stood and witnessed his disaster. We did not touch him, yet something fell on us from that teetering platform.

(2004)

THE FLUTE PLAYER

The Flute Player was the only picture I had in my kitchen in Berlin, at Ryke Strasse 27, in the back-courtyard building. I had hung it on the wall above the kitchen workbench. This bench was where I wrote – my workshop is how I thought of it at the time. With its heavy, rusting steel frame and four-metre-long wooden boards, it almost filled the room. On top of the boards rested the slightly chipped marble top of an old dressing table and it was on this that I actually wrote, pleasingly cool to my forearms as I worked there in the summer. It was even better if I put my pen down, turned my arms and pressed my wrists to the stone; it was almost a shock, a delightful coolness that penetrated my blood, ran up my back, my neck, and rippled over my scalp, palpating my skull like a precious helmet, the contours of which were just tangible there beneath the skin. For a few moments, I sat transfixed. That was when my gaze would fall on the image of the flute player and what I wished for was to live a life like his, in that house, on that hilltop, overlooking other houses, in a light that fell benevolently on everything, a life that seemed to have achieved a perfect balance.

Since my schooldays, Rik Wouters' painting had been kept in a folder with other reproductions of images. Our 'art master' – rather a fancy phrase for someone giving us art lessons in school – had handed each of us a folder and, during the course of the year, everyone was supposed to assemble their own little collection of examples of pictures from different periods. I had taken *The Flute*

Player to be the work of an Impressionist painter and, as far as I can remember, the art teacher never raised any objections. At the time, I neither knew who Rik Wouters was (I knew nothing of his short life), nor had ever heard of Fauvism.

1990: all my travelling in that particular year took me to France, mostly to the south, to one of the villages of the Languedoc, in the department of Hérault. It was precisely here that I imagined my new life unfolding. I would sit and write in one of those stone-built, sunlit houses, the very sight of which filled me with such confidence. I would simply have to despatch poems to my publisher on a regular basis and, perhaps, write something on the side for a newspaper and come evening, slowly and contentedly, I would drive my battered Ford Escort through the little villages down to the coast. I would take a walk along the shore, have a drink, or perhaps I would drive on to Montpellier to meet P . . . Every conceivable complication (actually, which publisher? what newspaper?) and all foreseeable difficulties – the foreign language, P's husband – seemed insignificant to me at the time. It was simply that the sudden, still wholly unfamiliar, almost startling possibility of living a life elsewhere triggered in me the most marvellous fantasies. And what do we take fantasies to be? They are plans; in 1990, the South of France was my plan.

It was not only the Mediterranean setting of such a fantasy that I recognised in the picture of the flute player. More than that, it was the easy-going, yet composed and serious figure presented by the young man, that air of calm and contemplation that I yearned for when I sat at my workbench on Ryke Strasse. I admired his autonomy. The calm way in which he pursued his art by letting it be and hence becoming more at ease with it. How to achieve that? How to get there? What were the secret pathways? How did one cross over into this mode of focused absence that was a prerequisite of poetry?

But there were other occasions as well. When I would come home around five o'clock in the morning from the Assel – the bar where, after the currency union, I earned a living, making no more than seven marks an hour – and I made the mistake of heading into the kitchen, to my workbench, instead of going straight to bed. Then it happened that the southern radiance enveloping the flute man would strike me as artifice, as not real. Then it was the black edges that caught my eye (the dark curtains to the left and right of the window) and the strange rigidity of his broad, angular tie which echoed the black of the curtains and hung from his neck like the heavy pendulum of a clock. Was it this perpendicular that dragged his gaze downwards? Had he put his flute down to listen to the noise of the machinery in his own chest, a sound he found difficult to reconcile with his music?

Then, there was no music from the flute; only silence filled the room. Only the sound of time. The man's silence was no accident, nor a blessing. Rather, it was an attitude, a way of sustaining himself there in the sunshine, with patience, with humility – there was a moment at which I came to see the picture in this way.

For several years, Wouters' image, hanging over my workbench, was an important point of reference for me, a reassurance. The flute player who is not playing. The one who pauses and goes deeper into himself. Just as he was gazing at a sheet of paper, or a book, with his head bowed (and his eyes closed?), I could stare at his image as I sat there, with my forearms pressed to the cool marble slab (a pulse on the stone), and contemplate a promise made to the future.

(2006)

THE INVOCATION

I can think of only one occasion when I actually spoke about 'Beauty'. It was at the request of Professor Winter, who filled his lectures on literary theory/aesthetics with a welter of quotations from Theodor Fontane. In my notes from that time, it is clear we were really attending lectures on Fontane and, more specifically, on Prussia, the aristocracy of the March of Brandenburg, and on decorum. As this continued, a gulf opened between him and us, the unsuspecting new students who, as happened every autumn, washed up in the lecture hall knowing next to nothing about manners or decorum, quite unfamiliar with what Professor Winter taught and embodied in his whole demeanour: the lifestyle of the Prussian squire.

This impression was reinforced by Winter's height, his finely chiselled profile, his impressive eloquence (marked with a slight lisp and nasal twang) and – whenever something needed a particular emphasis – his habit of lifting his long unibrow above the bridge of his nose in such a way that it resembled a little tent pitched on his forehead. Within this tent dwelled the sense of higher things, of honour, its codes. On the dais, Winter stood at the lectern and we gathered down below, squeezed onto wooden benches in a dilapidated lecture hall, either engrossed in taking notes, or laughing along with Winter's jokes – splendid jokes that confirmed his superiority and, in which all that was (yes, no doubt) decadent and ossified, yet all that was also charming, refined and utterly *exquisite* about Prussia (as embodied by Fontane's protagonists), triumphed over our own cultureless present. Even as Winter laughed, the little tent was being pitched. In a moment, his whole face would arrange itself in dozens of little wrinkles that somehow managed to focus attention on the little tent on his forehead. Winter's face became completely childlike when he laughed. I have hardly ever seen a more congenial face. And I admired Winter. Though he was quite clearly, to the very tips of his fingernails, engaged in the act of reproducing something, he was an original.

At any rate, it was Winter who conducted our oral examination in Aesthetics. It took place one dreary morning in a room with a balcony, in a medium-sized, run-down townhouse which served to accommodate two or three of the smaller departments in the Faculty of German Studies. Despite the cool weather, the balcony door stood open; the room was dim. I would have liked to turn the lights on. I could hardly make out Winter's face although, on the other hand, the gloom was comforting. Professor Winter said, 'Beauty, the Beautiful,' and I began speaking. Everything I had learned, one set piece after another, spanning the centuries. Winter sat there with his head bowed as if contemplating the desk before him. After a couple of minutes, he stood up from the desk and walked slowly across the room, then out onto the balcony. His steps were unhurried, without any obvious significance, nothing more than a matter-of-fact movement: a tall man exits a room and goes to stand on the balcony. The assistant, who was sitting, taking notes, half turned away on a chair at the end of the desk, nodded to me, which was clearly intended to mean: keep talking. But already, the fact that I could not make out the faces of my two examiners, that I had not yet had the chance to glean anything from their facial expressions, not even to catch some signs of encouragement, had left my speech feeling rather abandoned. Now, I floundered. When Winter left the room, I did not want to go on talking.

Yet the assistant, who was now suddenly alone in the room with me, nodded again, emphatically, encouragingly, though I stared uncertainly at her donkey-like nodding. Other than this, she showed no inclination to venture beyond her peripheral role. She kept the record; she noted down what I had to offer as I reeled off everything on the subject of Beauty. At least her neutrality helped me to think of her less as a person, even though I knew her, even though we spoke when we happened to meet in the street, or in a café, and even though we had slept together once – more by accident than intention, if such a thing can be said. I think a lot of things happened in just this way, at the time, in the student halls with their communal showers and shared kitchens. But here, in the half-light of my final examination in Aesthetics, I never gave it a thought: this was about my degree, about what I knew of 'Beauty', and she was there simply to take the minutes. Her role was no more than that laid down in the rubric of the exam regulations: she was an 'observer', not an interlocuter. And that reassured me.

Without really noticing, as I went on talking, I had gradually turned away from her. At the same time, as my presentation steadied and got underway again, I perhaps even raised my voice a little and, in the end, I was addressing the balcony door. Winter was only indistinctly visible through the reflections across the half-open, half-closed double doors of the balcony. He was evidently leaning, arms outstretched on the parapet, looking down into the garden and not moving. I had often stared down into this garden myself from a window in the stairwell. It was a beautiful old garden, the original, park-like layout of which was still quite visible beneath the uncultivated growth of more recent years. Whether Winter, out there on the balcony, could hear me talking, I did not know. He made no movement; he seemed exhausted. Could I go out and join him, staring down into the old garden for a while, still talking about Beauty? No. Should I just stop and be quiet? Perhaps. But

I went on speaking and gradually the awkwardness of the situation subsided and eventually vanished. I took in the scene: the balcony doors, a man standing on the balcony, completely absent, inside the room a woman sitting writing something at a desk, essentially absent, and my voice, dauntlessly discussing the Beautiful, a category of Aesthetics, clear and incomprehensible.

I began to listen to my own voice. Gradually, I began to perceive the scene without its actual content, its actual meaning. After all, my sentences were pre-prepared and the speech went on and on of its own accord. In the high-ceilinged room, which was barely furnished and, at first sight, had made such a dismal impression, I could make out a slight, almost imperceptible echo. My voice reverberated, it had a connection to this room and the room held and contained my voice. I was at ease here, alone with my voice. It was possible to go on and on talking and listening to myself. There was a great reassurance and satisfaction in this sensation. I was so at ease by now that I could no longer tell if my speech was in fact still about the Beautiful, its definitions from Plato to Baumgarten, Hegel, Ruge, Rosenkranz, Kant and Vischer, and, accompanying each name, a few sentences and additional observations that might suggest links to other aspects of the subject. One of them made reference to Tolstoy's essay, 'What is Art?' (without my ever having read it), another alluded to von Platen's poem 'Whoever looked at beauty with eyes . . .', and one quoted Hölderlin's closing sentence, 'Thus I thought', which probably called into question the entirety of his *Hyperion* – in short, I played the know-it-all. I had extracts in my head and something was dictating them from there into my own voice. But now that my voice had become wholly isolated in the room, it had taken on a life of its own. And it seemed as if, in its resounding isolation, it was giving me a picture of the walls, of the room, a picture of the man on the balcony, the woman at the desk. Yet it was merely talking to itself, accompanied by its own echo, which also seemed to originate in the things standing around it there. And when I came to – came back to myself – I remembered a moment of beauty:

From the gate to the cornerstone, I have just twenty metres. The gate, the driveway and the corner bring me to the cornerstone. The cornerstone protects the corner at the junction created by the driveway and the village road. The cornerstone is a boulder placed at the entrance to the farm and as a child I would stand there when I was on my own and boredom was getting the better of me, and I really could think of nothing to do. The cornerstone was my boundary stone. I was not supposed to venture beyond it, not alone. I would stand at the cornerstone and stare towards the village, past the pond sealed up beneath its duckweed. Mostly, I talked to myself – imaginary conversations with imagined companions. Actually, there were two girls, the Schuhmann twins, who sometimes came to our farm. They were three years older than me and made use of me in their mother-father-child games. One of the twins had to be the father – usually that was Kerstin. Andrea took the role of the mother, and I played the child. Andrea was a caring mother, though she could also be strict – I found both arousing. While Kerstin went out hunting in the backyard, I was raised by Andrea. Normally, before being put to bed, the child would have hurt something somewhere and Andrea would have to examine it carefully. A stomach ache and a girl's cool palm on my belly: there was nothing better. When Kerstin returned home with the kill, she would take me in her arms, which felt odd indeed: I was five years old and really too big and heavy for her. But it did not matter to Kerstin; the twins were powerful girls. What became of them, I do not know. But they never came often enough. And that is why I was sad as I stood on my own at the cornerstone.

At some point, I had begun to invoke the twins. In my childish imagination, I used the power of my voice to bridge the distance to the Schuhmanns' house which stood at the other end of the village. I imagined them hearing me as I called. I saw them interrupting their own games, then starting to run – and in a moment they would appear at the top of the incline beyond the pond. On one occasion, they really did appear: I stood there beside the corner-stone and yelled into the village and, laughing, the twins actually did appear. I never dreamed for a moment that it might have been a coincidence.

Sometimes it was Kerstin I called to, sometimes Andrea, always by turns and without ceasing. Kerstin was easier to call. There were just two syllables to her name that were clearly distinguished and could be shouted in sequence without any difficulty. And then 'Ahn-dreeeeeh-yaaaaahh' formed a kind of trisyllable. When I had been shouting this for a while and was already a bit hoarse, there were moments when I ran out of breath for her name, when it came to her name's final, long 'a', which in the part of the country where I grew up tends to get lengthened a good deal anyway, and also sinks into the murky depths somewhere between 'oh' and 'uu'. When I was a student, a speech therapist who gave a seminar on 'speech training' told me that all my vowels were 'creaky', in other words not clean, and she said this was pretty much 'irremediable'.

At the very end of my calling for Andrea, in those last, voiced moments before the drop back into silence, I made a discovery. The long-drawn-out, uncertain, increasingly breathless 'ah' sound – it reached down inside me, it trickled down into me. In this vocalised fragment that no longer travelled any distance at all beyond me towards the village, that no longer drowned out my own body with the desire to be heard in the Schuhmanns' house, I heard myself. This 'aaahh' dying of thirst in my throat, the gentle creaking of my vocal cords, had something warming about it as well as something wolfish. It only just filled my skull; it felt its way to the top of the dome as if creating it; it sounded my own inwardness – without my thinking at all in such terms as 'skull' or 'inwardness'. Yet I remember the extraordinary sensation of suddenly being close to myself and feeling myself more clearly defined. It was a first sense of self, and the sensation was that of being in the world with a body of my own, a distinct body of my own that I could make creak when I shouted. So, for ages then, I would just shout for Andrea, listening closely to the slow strangling of my voice at the close of her name, a sound we would more likely associate – without any further visual clues – with the feeble-minded or those close to death. I prolonged this sound for as long as I had breath; I tickled the wolf in its den. That is why I think of Andrea today when people talk of an 'inner voice'. Andrea, with whom I made the discovery of this wolfish rattle, this wonderful-sounding growling in the skull.

But in keeping with my childish sense of fairness, I soon started to call out for Kerstin again. But with her name it was different. Unlike calling to Andrea, calling to Kerstin came wholly from me, it had a quite different sense of trajectory. I liked the 'K' from which I could launch off cleanly, then came the flight of the drawn-out 'ehhhrr', which I allowed to land and vibrate on a kind of high wire, though when it quivered, it became a throaty 'ahhh' at extreme amplitudes. It sounded captivatingly ugly, and I found it hard to stop. With Kerstin's name, I grew conscious of a connectedness to the village, to the environment that I was filling with sound.

I do not know if anyone was watching while I called out to the village. Unimaginable that someone would come over to explain that Andrea and Kerstin were out of earshot. Part of this calling was that the village remained completely silent and unresponsive. If someone did walk by, I let out just a few calls. I probably seemed crazy, but I was just a child and so not entirely rational. Since usually no one came along, I could carry on shouting for ages.

I enjoyed shouting. It is possible that while shouting I forgot that I was actually shouting for someone, and I also forgot what it was I was shouting. All the time, while the phonetic forms of 'Andrea' or 'Kerstin' ran through me, I had the village in view and the village was my world, what I knew. I knew it and yet there was something happening to it: the calling changed what could be seen, it transformed the place.

To begin with, the village was a kind of desert, a featureless place with a pond, a house, fences and the absence of any response. All round me: the bare wasteland. In my childish imagination, it was a prairie, the steppes, virtually uninhabited, a silent region across which my calling could spread itself, lose itself unhindered. There stood a chieftain who had lost his people, the last of the Mohicans, crying his lament to the winds. In this solitude, my call, in all its uniqueness, had the possibility of being heard by myself, sometimes as a curious melody, sometimes as just a disorganised fragment of sound; a rough scrap of sound that could be launched out across the steppe over and over again.

When I think of how often I stood at the cornerstone in those days to shout – apparently it was no longer just about the wish for Andrea's hand on my belly, or for Kerstin's paternal tenderness. I had discovered a distinct pleasure in the invocation itself. There was something about certain sounds flowing pleasingly through me, so that there were times when I would stand on tiptoe, I would lift my head and the sky came into view with its scattering of clouds on which I hung with my sounds. And I saw my surroundings change around me. The invocation built its own resonating chamber, it irrigated the wasteland, it built half-timbered houses with people in them who sat at the table and swayed and lived according to the rhythm of the invocation. It was I who gave life to this steppe and that life had the rhythms of my endless calling to Kerstin and Andrea. The whole beautiful world of the village was a unique self-portrait – not of myself, but of my calling out, an answer without answer.

As I have said, the invocation transformed the place. The half-timbering of the houses opposite, the clay crumbling from the barn walls, the picket fences, the silvery willows around the pond, the pond itself, the washing on the lines, the bend of the road, the fire station – these things no longer appeared to me in isolation. They showed me they belonged together, that together they composed a picture and that this picture was utterly coherent. It emanated from me and my calling out; it was in perfect unison with me and my alternating call, the original meaning of which, in search of a reply and ultimately a release from my solitude, had grown from and transcended its two tangible addressees, namely Kerstin and Andrea. From my cornerstone, I sang of the place, my world, my solitude and the experience of my own voice with what the names of the twins had given my voice by way of sonic materials. This is what I remembered in the course of my examination with Winter. My calling, this plaintive and contented singsong about absence, had turned into an invocation whose reverberations in the image of the place – of my infant world – and its echoing within myself had combined to create a moment of extraordinary beauty.

(2005)

IN THE MOVIE BUNKER

1.

It started with the poster – the wording framed in black, not unlike an obituary. Year after year, it was displayed at railway stations, at bus stops and on trees along the streets. The headline read '*Musterung*', followed in bold by the year of birth of those who were being summoned. As a child, I thought I knew well enough what the word '*Musterung*' meant – 'pattern'. It was a word almost entirely associated for me with the plastic cloth on our kitchen table, with its dull sheen and pale blue check pattern that every morning took my tired eyes hostage. But for what or for whom was this 'pattern' being announced on the poster?

Then the posters would vanish; I forgot about them and, one year on, they would reappear again, displayed on the churchyard wall beside the path I had to walk along at least once every day. There was some obligation here that no one was able to escape – that much I already understood: something was going to be unavoidable, but the years being referred to (the 1950s) were unimaginably distant in the past. It was only when the year 1960 showed up on one of these posters – and thus my own decade had been broached – that I persuaded myself to stop and stand in front of it.

'Attendance is due on . . .', 'You must bring with you . . .', 'In the event of failure to attend . . .', and so on. The words had the kind of seriousness that frightened me: no chance of escape. From an early age, I was disposed to believe in such a possibility – a system of repression that made it possible for me to feel pretty much carefree for long periods of time. Because of this my mother often used to say I was 'happy-go-lucky', but that was not really true because, fundamentally, I sensed the threat perfectly clearly, yet my home-spun insouciance sought to draw an immediate veil over it. She was mistaken – but the unreasonable demands of the real world could actually be made to vanish for remarkably long periods of time with the help of this cloak of invisibility.

One of the phrases on the poster – the 'District Conscription Office' – impressed me (it still impresses me today). It had the ring of a genuine military operation. I was seventeen years old when the year of my own birth, 1963, appeared on the posters. On 6 April 1981, I walked into the District Conscription Office, thereby obeying the very first command of my time as a soldier.

I can see the date in my 'Health Record'. The health record book was begun on the day of recruitment and – this was the intention – it was updated throughout the remainder of my military career. Stages in your life were recorded there according to phases or categories of fitness. As a soldier in the National People's Army, you progressed through various kinds of deployment appropriate to your age and physical condition. On 4 April 1986, at the time of the final entry in my health record, twenty-seven of the thirty-eight possible 'service categories' still remained available to me.

In some ways, the brown card-bound health record is my very first diary. Although strictly military and medical in character, some of the entries contain details that I find astonishing today. Entry for 7 February 1984: 'On 31.1. several slabs fell on the pat.'s lower back / lumbar x-ray / urinalysis.' What slabs? I remember none of it.

When soldiers were discharged from military service, the health record was entrusted to them 'for personal safekeeping' until the next call-up. To ensure nothing untoward occurred, there were 'Instructions for the Safekeeping of the Health Record' printed inside its card cover: three paragraphs in small font and three more on what you were expected to do, divided into further points and sub-points, including the proper treatment of what was referred to as 'medical resources', which included the gas-mask goggles that were supposed to be retained by their owner after active service and be appropriately maintained, protected and kept at the ready. According to Section 3, Sub-section 2, Paragraph a), the gas-mask goggles were to be 'brought with you to each new call-up to military service'. Otherwise, any use of them was prohibited, though some of my friends disregarded this because the little plastic frames with straps to go round the ears, reminiscent of rubber bands, would never slip off your head when you were playing football. When we caught sight of a striker wearing gas-mask goggles, it was impossible not to think of Wolfgang Borchert, who we read enthusiastically in our first year at university: 'You call those spectacles? I think you're being deliberately odd.'

I have mostly forgotten what else happened on that first day at the District Conscription Office. I do remember my readiness to comply with the almost cheerful tone of command that prevailed there. Perhaps I wanted to show that I was not stupid and that I already understood what all this was about. I was certainly hoping that, after the process was over, all this would disappear again as quickly as possible under the cover of my invisibility cloak.

I do still remember that the '*Musterung*', the summoning to medical examination for military service, started with the presentation of the ID cards we had been told to bring with us. Then there was a long wait in the corridor, perhaps two, maybe three hours. A first brief interview was followed by a series of medical checks as we processed from room to room, at one point having to strip down to our underpants. I was pleased to have remembered to put on gym shorts that morning and looked on in silent triumph at the other hapless guys standing in their baggy fine-rib briefs.

I was measured and I was weighed. I had to hop on one leg across the room, to stand up straight, to bend forwards, and so on. In the hearing test, I managed 'whispered speech at six metres', or so it tells me in my health record. And, although I knew what was coming (because of countless stories embellished with obscenities), I was still shocked at the end by the swift, firm grasp of my pants, a hand gripping my balls and toying with them, the testicles and epididymis, a practised hand that took four, maybe five seconds, foreskin back, no restrictions and, as for the rest, 'All there!' The uniformed doctor dictated something of the sort across the room and the nurse sitting behind him conscientiously wrote it down. She was at a school desk in the middle of the room and, without glancing up, she recorded everything in her small, careful hand in the health record. At first glance, I took her for a student.

But most of the doctor's speech remained incomprehensible. The tone in which it was spoken also deprived me of my last hope of a miracle. The night-time sleepwalking – which I had made report of because it was said to be on the legendary list of grounds that might prove sufficient to declare a conscript 'permanently unfit for service' – was received without so much as a flicker of interest from the senior physician, Dr Seyfarth (I can still read his name; I can see his rubber stamp).

In fact, it had taken some considerable effort for me to broach the issue because, there behind me, barefoot like me and well within earshot, a whole line of recruits was waiting for the conclusion of the examination. I felt immediately ashamed of something I had simply made up. As it turned out, no reference to it ever made its way into my health record.

At the time, I had no idea what it took to make a story credible. The story of the sleepwalker probably reached Dr Seyfarth's ears many times every day. It was precisely because 'The Sleepwalker' featured on the notional list of supposedly successful stories that I really ought to have tried to tell it differently. Thomas Mann's *Confessions of Felix Krull, the Confidence Trickster* might have served as a guide, but then not everybody is capable of faking an epileptic seizure. Anyway, I did not know anything of this or of any other books – literature did not interest me. It was only in the army that I started to read.

So, while I tried to keep my voice steady and detailed my supposedly restless and risky sleepwalking tendencies, some of those in the queue behind me were trying to shake off their own nerves, or sense of shame, by chattering and sniggering, though they were immediately reprimanded by one of the officers who continually patrolled the rooms. With these fellow sufferers breathing down my neck, the bark of the officers and the blank face of Dr Seyfarth (I wonder whether he, the doctor, is still alive and, if so, whether he sometimes thinks of that age of the sleepwalkers?), under the circumstances, it was not easy to tell any story. Sure, in the tales of the Arabian Nights, the danger is on a completely different scale, but then, the setting is ideal by comparison: a candlelit quiet room, curtains, quilts and cushions, silk or velvet covers, and finally, a very attentive listener . . .

By contrast, the rooms of the District Conscription Office were brightly lit, and the lino shone so much that it hurt your eyes. After a while, my feet grew cold on the floor which had evidently been recently polished or coated with a special wax. If you stood in one place for any length of time, the soles of your bare feet started to stick to the floor. Those waiting in line, as they spontaneously shifted from one leg to the other, made a soft, slight smacking sound. After a while, it began to sound as if paper or something was being continually torn up or, at least, something was once and for all, in the course of that day, losing its currency. In the end, confronting the recruitment panel of four officers and their questions, I found myself possessed of neither great courage, nor a good story. What little courage I had was enough to refuse the longer period of service (three years or more, instead of eighteen months) and to decline service at the border: 'I just don't think I could shoot anyone' – that was enough, even in the absence of a story, everyone knew that.

2.

My nervousness increased by stages. At one point, I could no longer cross the station square without thinking of 1 November, the day on which I was to be called up. Before I stepped onto the station concourse, my gaze was inexorably drawn off to the right, towards the sidings of the marshalling yard. There, on one of the tracks, was the ramp in front of which soldiers from Gera and its surrounds were required to assemble.

A few months earlier, at five in the morning, I had accompanied my friend S there. A large group of men with travelling bags had already gathered in front of the ramp. The whole scene was illuminated by the headlights of a couple of lorries whose engines were idling. Somewhere on the way across the station square, I had the sense of losing my friend. He said goodbye with a quick hug, stepped across an invisible line and was gone. Yet, all the while, I could see him perfectly well. But I noticed how his back stiffened, his stride shortened, his walk adapting itself to the different rules that applied on the other side. Just in front of the ramp, he turned round again: he waved to me, or rather, he thrust his left arm into the air. It looked awkward and, at the same time, as if he wanted to give me a show of defiance. Even as he was doing this, he was already being dazzled by the headlights. 'Cigarettes out!'

was the last thing I heard, then I too gave a wave, turned around and drove home.

3.

The leap down from the lorry: I tried hard not to betray any sense of clumsiness. Perhaps ten or fifteen officers stood at the entrance to a compound surrounded by barbed wire which had to be the barracks. So far, I had seen nothing more than a dismal display of wood and brick huts.

'Compan-eeee – close order!' A few of us knew what this meant, but it took a while before we were all standing in our rows of three. I noticed the officers' faces, some looking tense, some amused. Yet everything proceeded quietly enough. There was a short, rather slap-dash alcohol inspection for which we had to step forwards with our luggage. For a few minutes, nothing could be heard but the passing of cars on the nearby road. A big chimney with the lettering 'VEB Leuna' rose from the factory premises on the other side of the road.

'Bags – pick hup!' The command had been shouted, perhaps inadvertently, by several officers at the same time, that is, not prop-erly synchronously, so that to begin with I did not catch what had actually been said, though I noticed how everyone instantly shoul-dered their travelling bags. Some were even carrying suitcases, though these had been expressly forbidden in the conscription order. The next command was similarly incomprehensible. Straight away, that fear again: of not understanding quickly enough, or even not understanding at all what was going to be required in this strange place. An ear-splitting whistle cut through the air and a flame burst from the Leuna chimney across the way.

We passed through the gate – a framework of steel tubing over which some barbed wire had been draped crosswise and rather carelessly. The gate was freshly painted but still managed to look run-down and bodged together. Just a few metres along the road between the huts, one of the officers (Sergeant Bade, as we later learned) began to give us a marching rhythm: left, left, left-two-three-four. In Bade's muffled voice and with the way he tried to maintain a low register, the whole thing sounded more like 'let, let, let-hoo-hee-hoor', which is probably why two or three of the guys started laughing. A murmuring arose which was promptly yelled down by a second sergeant. As if none of this was out of the ordinary, this sergeant, in his impressively polished boots, strode on across the grassed areas running alongside the road to the barracks.

The effort to stay in step while also managing our bags and suitcases resulted in ludicrous hopping and shambling around. But the strangest thing was the steam: a soft, white vapour that welled up out of the ground on all sides, from gaps in the concrete surface of the road, from cracks in the pavements between the huts, and, in some places, this vapour also rose like a marvellous mist from patches of grass. The sergeant with his shiny boots marched through it, seemingly unconcerned. Black, polished leather, misted by water vapour – when I think back, that is my first impression of this time.

Introduction to Hut Six, Dormitory Ten: seven iron double bunk beds, fourteen cupboards, one broom cupboard, fourteen stools, one table. It was the room at the far end of the corridor, facing the room occupied by Sergeant Zaika – an enemy, as it turned out. On the other hand, the other thirteen men in my quarters seemed like friends from the start.

In the hours that followed, we passed through the maze of clothing and equipment huts. By the afternoon, everyone was dressed in their basic uniform. We were given soup and tea in a low building close to the gate. From there, we marched back down the road to a large bunker-like building. It was a huge, semicircular structure with a distinct crack running across the top. To my surprise, there was a cinema inside the building, or at least there was a screen and several rows of folding chairs, and soon after I heard the term 'movie bunker' for the first time.

The movie bunker was surprisingly spacious. Just a few moments after we had taken our seats, the lights went down. I was thankful for the darkness. I can hardly remember anything about the film. There were tanks and other armaments; there was no end of talk about peace and the difficult, but necessary, task of fighting for it, which meant defending it (by whatever means necessary). I had begun to close my eyes when someone touched me on the shoulder. It was the sergeant with the misty boots. He did not say anything, but I understood I was to get up. As I did so, my shadow fell across the screen and got mixed up there with images of a prison camp. Then the film was showing a city completely destroyed by war. In amongst the ruins, on bended knee, a Red Army soldier was waving the flag of the Soviet Union, just as my shadow was slipping away beneath him.

The sergeant and I walked back towards a row of long, thin lights. For a moment, I glimpsed the soldier who was standing behind the film projector. He looked calm and I admired him for that – for his long-term familiarity with all this, for having, as it seemed to me, survived it. There were mirrors on the wall at the back of the bunker. In front of the mirrors stood large chairs with metal armrests, head rests and height-adjustable seats. It was largely because of my state of mind, but what these objects suggested to me were electric chairs. In fact, they were nothing other than what you would find in a barber's shop: big, wide chairs, upholstered in army-green leather. The seats were cracked, and the backs shone greasily in the glare of the neon tube lighting that hung on long rails from the ceiling of the bunker.

Behind the big chairs there were wooden benches for waiting. They were already taken, so I had to stand. The lockers between the washbasins, as well as the tiles above them, were painted green. An older, more thickset officer moved between the hairdressing chairs and was gesticulating. He seemed very annoyed, obviously wondering why the barbers had not yet begun their work. This was Captain Buddrus, head of the so-called Technology Park, which is where I came across him later, on my countless days spent there, and also while I was training as a driver of a W50 Ballon, a truck with unusually wide tyres.

The barbers' clippers in action made a kind of chattering noise that drowned out the film. It was nice when they were eased up the back of your neck, but more nerve-wracking round the ears. The barbers all wore white rubber aprons over their uniforms as if they had just popped in from the kitchen or the canteen. It was clear they were not trained barbers, but they were proficient with the little trimmers and, like the soldier behind the projector, they were at least half a year, some an unbelievable whole year, of army camp experience ahead of us. The evening before my call-up, my mother had cut my hair. Squeezed in the aisle between the built-in cupboards in our new kitchen: first I had to swivel to the left for the right side, then right for the left side. With a hand mirror held up in front of me, I had agonised over every millimetre cut off – completely pointlessly, as it now turned out.

The barber bent my ear forwards and said something I did not hear. The noise of the clippers was too loud. I smelled his breath and, for the first time, caught a whiff of the disinfectant used to wash soldiers' clothes at the military laundry in Merseburg. Once a fortnight, laundry was delivered and, sooner or later, the disinfectant triggered a fierce red, horribly itchy rash between the legs – then you needed ointment. The ointment was dispensed at the infirmary; it was cortisone which we applied in great quantities over the following months. There was never any consideration of possible side effects, nor did we much care as long as there was something to soothe the burning on the insides of our thighs.

I said 'Uh-huh' or 'Oh yeah' while the barber used my uniform jacket collar to steady the clippers, running them round my neck as if on a rail. Under the gown, between my knees, I had hold of my uniform cap; it felt odd to be wearing headgear again. The cap made my head feel as it used to when I was a child: winter holidays, ski trips, marks on my forehead and ears, or the hat pulled right down over my face, the way it gradually frosted up with my breath freezing in the wool . . . Cut hair was piling up all round the chairs and the barbers waded through it in their boots.

The roar of artillery fire rose behind me. Staring into the mirror, I was part of the film: tanks trundled over a lumpy terrain and at the same time across my face, pale under the fluorescent lights. The barrels of guns swung left and right – as did my startled expression. 'The armed forces gearing up to advance . . .' For a moment, it seemed possible to bring the whole thing tumbling down with hardly more than a twitching of the corner of my mouth. From his place on the sofa, a big heavy, crocheted blanket across his knees, my grandfather would shout, 'Tanks, my boy, nothing but mobile coffins!' – and he was one who ought to know. In the mirror, I stared at my own face. Under the chattering of the clippers, for the first time, I found a few moments' peace. But I could not wholly abandon the effort to follow something of the plot or the commentary of the film being shown. I thought there was perhaps something in it that we would be quizzed on later, something that might prove important in some way to my survival in this new environment. 'Our air force, equipped with the most advanced technology . . .'

'Stop, now stop! On to the picture!' At the captain's command, the clippers fell silent. Off to one side, to the left of the barbers' waiting area, another queue had started to form, stretching forwards into a barely lit part of the bunker. The line of recruits ended in front of a wooden cubicle, the narrow door of which opened and shut at regular intervals.

It was only when I was sitting on the stool in the glare of the lamp that shone warmly on my face that I noticed the photographer was a woman. Instantly, I felt embarrassed at the sight I presented: the stiff, new uniform, the newly cropped skull. And I felt a dislike of the sergeant who was assisting her, even though he had spoken to me with some friendliness, or, at least, in a rather different tone from Bade or Buddrus. But that had more to do with her than with me — that much I understood immediately.

The photographer said something to me. I think she said, 'Look this way, please!' In her right hand, she had raised a pen in the air. Before she vanished completely again behind her camera, I noticed she had dark hair and was still quite young. She was not wearing a uniform and yet, here she was, in the movie bunker. I gazed up at her small pale hand holding the pen. It was a ballpoint pen.

Today, when I look at my military service ID card with its laminated dog tag, I see that glance up towards the pen and the hand that remained perfectly still in the air, the slim pale hand of the photographer with her baton as she conducted the moment. 'Thank you!' – perhaps she said thank you, perhaps not. The hand was then lowered, and for a moment I was left staring into a void. Out of that void, there emerged the uniform of the sergeant who was already ushering me out and calling the next person in to face the camera. For the first time since arriving at the camp, I felt exhausted and depressed.

The photograph on my ID card ('Photograph in Uniform') which, to this day, I keep in a kind of 'life-box' along with my health record and other bits and pieces from the past, in fact tells a rather different story. There, I am smiling a little and my head is inclined to the right as if quietly questioning. The arches of the eyebrows and the heart-shaped line of the upper lip, if you look closely, are softly delineated and everything seems peaceable enough. On the other hand: the smile sits as if tied to the corners of the mouth. And the eyelids are lowered a little, giving the face an expression of detachment and distrust. What you see are two quite different expressions on the same face in the same instant. It is impossible to tell who I was at that moment. The only thing that is easy to see is that the person in the photo is trying, as best he can, to hide his distress.

The longer I go on gazing at the picture, the more unclear things become. In the end, all I am feeling is sadness, regret – and self-pity. And then, finally, I am angry at everything that led to my ending up in that bunker, my bare face before the flash of the camera, completely at its mercy and struggling to maintain my composure with a strange and, it now strikes me, quite useless pride.

When I look at my ID card again a few days later, the sense of perspective in relation to the whole situation seems, for a moment, to have changed: suddenly, there is the twenty-year-old soldier staring back at me. There is some irritation and yet the impression is strong, undeniable, and I give in, I go along with it, and immediately the question arises as to whether, back then, thirty-five years ago, he could have seen me with those slightly narrowed eyes, while his gaze was fixed on the lifted hand holding the writing implement: a glimpse into the future – and hence his smile? The thought instantly yields a sense of parity between him and me and my anger begins to subside. Wasn't that expression on his face one of solidarity and understanding? I – from then – was encouraging me – from now – to peer all the way back into that wooden cubicle with the photographer and the sergeant, back to the barber's in the movie bunker, back to the day of conscription, the day of recruitment, back to the poster announcing the year 1963 in its funereal lettering, back to the embarrassment felt in the instant of the photograph. Fleetingly, I recognise the outline of a truth composed entirely of the soft, unyielding stuff of patience: life is about patience. It is about the meaning, for which everything that has happened to us, at one time or another, is patiently waiting.

(2012, 2018)

THE SOGGY HEMS OF HIS SOVIET
TROUSERS: IMAGE AS A WAY INTO
THE NARRATION OF THE PAST

At the start of 2011, we moved and went to live for almost a year at the Villa Massimo in Rome. All I wanted to do was write. Writing at last, and there would be time enough for it finally, a long, undisturbed period to devote to it with no other obligations, no need to travel. The evening we arrived, I sat in my ten- or twelve-metre-high studio, a large echoing room with a facade full of windows and no end of light, to set about it at last: my novel. A novel bathed in Roman light with a vista of melancholy pines and cypresses, though to have nothing more than a reading lamp on a desk would have been enough; 'my lamp and my blank paper', as Gaston Bachelard so aptly describes: 'The right place for solitary work is a circle of lamplight in a small room.'[8] But my Roman workspace had originally been designed for sculptors, sculptors of a hundred years ago, mind you, who were then still working on equestrian statues, massive sculptures and groups of figures. After a week, I pushed the few pieces of furniture that were there into a kind of cubbyhole in one corner of the room and I ended up sitting myself down behind a cupboard. It was a decent, half-height, double-doored cupboard that I could also make use of as a store for my working materials. And yes, for the first few months of our stay, I basically just sat there, behind a cupboard, trying not to notice Rome. If, back then, I had read the German-Roman writer, Marie Luise Kaschnitz, for example, I might have been forewarned: 'You try to reflect on yourself, unearthing what you've brought – more than half a lifetime of experiences and memories – only to watch in horror as these treasures slip through your hands.'[9]

What I had brought with me amounted to fourteen removal boxes filled with books, folders, photocopies, research and working materials that I had gathered over the previous year, including plot sketches, chapter drafts, character dossiers and dramatic scripts, as well as three fleshed-out openings to the novel that had come from experimenting with a variety of narrative perspectives. To be honest, the word 'experimenting' suggests a kind of competence I did not really possess. Fourteen boxes of books and some travel bags packed into the footwell with the back seat folded down – that is about as much as a Volvo V50 can hold. With this on board, I had navigated across the Alps, travelling south – the Brenner Pass, an overnight stay in Bolzano, then onwards until, at some point, there had been a sudden shift in the quality of the light. In places it was almost dazzling, as if someone had switched on an extra lamp. It started near the junction of the A13 beyond Padua but, really, I did not have eyes for it, no eyes for the south: I wanted the novel and did not want to fail. My luggage was well stocked with wool and there was a knitting pattern in my head – or so I thought.

At the Villa Massimo, in the course of their so-called 'shop talks', I presented the three openings to my novel. In the otherwise mostly German-speaking Villa, the 'shop talk' is the name they have given to what are really preliminary presentations, a kind of getting-to-know-you initial meeting. What happens during these 'shop talks' is that the whole group of residential Fellows, plus the Villa Massimo crew – that includes the director, his wife, the staff, the caretakers and the Roman gardeners – all process from studio to studio, over the course of a morning, and each Fellow talks about himself and his work. This took place about a month after my arriving in Rome. The fact that I had not actually accomplished anything during that first month of labour behind the cupboard had to be quietly brushed aside. Three openings to a novel, plus fourteen boxes of raw materials, all of it now scattered decoratively across several tables and the studio floor, easily produced an impression of abundance, of hard work and creativity. At least as important, this 'shop talk' was also the right moment to show all the other, no doubt hard-working, no doubt extraordinarily productive Fellows that you too were doing fine, that things were rolling along about as well as could be expected. Besides that, it was also a signal to my pleasant, always friendly 'Letteratura' colleague – I mean the other writer in our little community of arts practitioners. He was a poet who, daily, set out on tours of discovery, exploring this 'quite fantastical', this 'great', more often this 'really great', or, on the other hand, 'magnificent' and always 'unbelievable' city of Rome, the place I had yet seen so little of.

Just a short while later, everything lay in ruins. The novel was resisting, indeed it categorically refused. At the same time, there was the Villa's programme of events: carefully thought-through recommendations, plus other ideas from the artistic director, group visits to Caravaggio, concerts in the Villino, excursions to Olevano, film screenings in the Villa's main building, and so on – all perfectly delightful, though not for one who simply is not writing. The one who cannot write has no interest in any programme of events, certainly no excursions and, above all, he has no desire to meet up with other creative artists. Right now, to be in residence with other artists is not what he wants . . . Already, each morning I was staring with tired eyes at a blank page, and I was becoming more and more anxious. Sometimes I pulled out this folder from my cupboard, sometimes that one, and then I would frantically leaf through my notes. Those early morning hours were especially important because the Villa's two gardeners would start up their deafening work in the grounds at around 10 a.m. Particularly dreadful were the electric hedge trimmers and the lawn mower, built like a tractor, which the smaller, chubbier gardener would manoeuvre across the lawns in interminable circles.

What had happened? I had set out to write a novel, my first novel. And my idea was that the post-reunification years in Berlin would be very promising material, or more exactly, my own experiences of that period. Until 1993, I had lived and worked in Berlin as a bricklayer, postman and post-grad German Studies student, but above all as a bartender and kitchen help in a bar called the Assel on Oranienburger Strasse in the Mitte district of Berlin. In my Roman writing project, my intention was to progress with this in a more systematic way, with more sense of structure, as would suit the sheer scale of my ambition. I thought in particular that it would be an issue of rising to the requirements of a novel. With that in mind, I had collected a wealth of materials that included not just letters, photos, notes and writing experiments dating back to that period, but also documents of all kinds, such as tenancy and subtenancy agreements, applications for housing benefit, electricity and gas bills, my first contract with Deutsche Telekom from 1990, my telephone number, its tariff, even the colour of my first telephone (anthracite). I had also had conversations with friends from that time, contemporary eyewitnesses as it were, who had responded to questions, and I had written down what came to light. As well as this, I had been dishing out tasks and instructions to remember – to my parents, for example. My mother was to recall the work she used to do on my grandfather's farm, as well as her first typewriter – all good material for flashbacks, or so I thought. My father fulfilled his given task to recall the details of his first car, a Russian model called a Zhiguli, a precursor of the Lada. Actually, he enjoyed this so much that he produced a thirty-page document, most of which consisted of a close detailing of mechanical faults and how they had been successfully resolved – none of it proving to be especially dramatic. I also talked at length to my parents about their move to the West, the story of which was intended to form a subplot in my novel.

However, at the heart of all this preparatory work was my own research on the city of Berlin and the so-called 'Berlin Literature' which, alone, filled four of my fourteen boxes. Two other key areas in this research were the Russian mafia and the 'service dog system'. In pursuit of my research into the history of the service dog system, especially details of the breeding and training of border guard dogs in the former border dog camp at Wilhelmshorst (the dilapidated buildings of which stood just a few hundred metres from where I was then living), I hired a German language and literature student from Freiburg, who copied several hundred pages for me from the military archives there, a branch of the Federal Archives. You've guessed it – the mafia and the history of the border dogs, before and after the fall of Communism, were going to play a significant role in the novel. That was the plan. And did I ever have a plan! There were sketches of the structure of the text, plot outlines, details of the contents of individual chapters and, best of all, a timetable. For this schedule, I had drawn up a chart, a timeline on which I could see at a glance when any particular chapter was going to be drafted, revised and completed. This fateful little pencil diagram was tacked up on the inside of the door of the cupboard behind which I sat to write – or, not to put too fine a point on it, had hoped to write.

These days, I would compare my methods at the time to a large Russian rocket that requires three stages to escape Earth's gravity. Phase 1: the work of reconstruction and visualisation – preparation of experiential materials, a kind of memory machine.

The documents, especially, promised the possibility of such a reconstruction, a plethora of authentic starting points, plus the promise of the so-called first-hand experience. Phase 2: literary transformation, elaboration and refinement. Phase 3: igniting the literary high points by means of imagination, particular devices, the stylistic and linguistic crafts. And then, successful flight . . . or so I thought. But my mission never escaped the Massimo cosmodrome. Nothing worked. Even the material (Phase 1) was impossible to harvest to any great effect. There were two problems. Firstly, the material seemed completely uninteresting and obviously tired – like those bouts of fatigue to the verge of unconsciousness, the kind of sudden paralysis I experienced years ago at school and again, later, in the reading rooms of particular archives. Everything I read seemed grey and dull as the paper it was written on. Secondly, the materials had the kind of hypnotic effect you might expect from, say, four hundred pages on the 'service dog system'. Among these, to take one example, there was the pedigree of a German Rottweiler, named Berry von der Schweizerhütte, a dog that had been bought by Lieutenant Colonel Muschwitz, a vet in the National People's Army, with the intention of training it as a border dog, at the cost of 300 marks, which had been paid to a breeder in Neubrandenburg by Post Office cashier's cheque. Berry's career would lure me into the bottomless pit of the remote world of the past. For days on end, I would go whirling through the vortex of the story of a border dog without being able to come up with anything useful for my novel. In the end, only the aristocratic names that featured in Berry's pedigree, Berry's ancestors as immortalised in the stud book, buzzed around my head: Tell von Vogelhaus, Frei von Peenestrom, Fred von Falkenbruch, Ondra von Hildakloster, Cilla von Teufelskreis, and so on. And yet, there were also Berry's early days in Neubrandenburg, the demands of his training at the border dog camp in Wilhelmshorst and, from there, to the Berlin Wall and, following the fall of the Wall, his continued travels across murky canals and into the West, to Mannheim (former border dogs were popular because they still had their bite, as it was said in breeder circles, particularly Rottweilers). I pursued all this as if entranced by it. The material had its own appeal, the fascination of the factual was powerful, but it had absolutely nothing to give to my writing. And so it turned out for all the other assembled materials, the documents, the interviews, the archives. The stuff of the past absorbed me, and I was soon completely exhausted – but exhausted to no end. Despite this, I forced myself on; I worked. I wrote three, perhaps four chapters, but the whole thing remained colourless and sounded contrived. Phase 2 did not ignite, and Phase 3 was out of the question.

Rome, Roma – I could have read in Kaschnitz: 'every incanta-tion begins with the uttering of a name'.[10] And Rome, Roma, *Roman* (meaning 'novel' in German) – didn't that sound like an almost natural step up? Instead, crisis. Heart palpitations, a high temper-ature, night sweats, sleeplessness, stomach cramps, high blood pressure – what followed was the swift deployment of the complete spectrum of my tendencies to hypochondria, as exaggerated as comparing the failure of a novel to the collapse of the Colosseum, which, in Roman superstition, foretells the fall of Rome and, in consequence, the end of days and ruination of the whole world: ridiculous – and no, of course, no comparison. And yet – the writer who does not write is completely worthless, is nothing, particularly to himself. 'Fuck Rome, fuck the Villa Massimo'[11] – if I had read Kaschnitz I would also have read those words, which is how she sums up the mood of the resident Fellows of her day. I would have discovered that she herself was such a Fellow and that she had written Roman poems and played *bocce* 'among the smells of decay and the cool shade' – her description of the Villa in her book *Places* (*Orte*).

But I had not written anything, and I had not even played *bocce*. I had just sat behind the cupboard for a long time, getting no sleep at night, hating the city and its din, the roar of the traffic, the ambulance sirens from the nearby Policlinico, the Vespa alarms set wailing by every passing gust of wind and not silenced for what remained of the night. Then the rubbish collections at four o'clock in the morning when the droning dustcart circled the Villa and the unparalleled, thunderous clattering of the empty bottles that struck like a thump in the kidneys. But there was never silence in my studio either. From the room below, the thin, irritating whistle of a radiator penetrated the night, and from above, a knocking upstairs: tapping noises around midnight, the ghosts of our predecessors, those who had also never achieved peace (or so I fancied as my heart raced frantically), all those ghostly Fellows also hounded by the roster of their own, never finished work, of novels never completed . . .

Such were the nights. What then followed were visits to the doctor. From a list of doctors working in Rome in collaboration with the German Embassy, I found Dr Wallbrecher. On my way to consult Wallbrecher, with tired eyes and jangling nerves, I caught sight of Rome for the first time since we had arrived. I took the 62 bus from the Piazza Bologna to the Vatican and from there hurried uphill towards number 30 on the Via Domenico Silveri. In other words, as the sun shone brilliantly in the blue sky, I passed close to St Peter's Square where the canonisation of Pope John Paul II was being prepared and I caught a half-glimpse of St Peter's Basilica, its cupola floating high above everything else. Even now, when I think of that day, my hurrying to see Dr Wallbrecher, I can still feel it – that fear of life disguised as a fear of death, in the midst of which I sped past the most 'fantastical' views in Rome.

Wallbrecher's practice consisted of many small rooms hung with oil paintings. In the waiting room, there was a still life with books lying open. Books with curling pages on which vases stood, or clocks had been left – evidently, these were books no one read anymore. Alongside this hung a licence to practise medicine, issued in Munich. Dr Wallbrecher looked as exhausted as I felt. To start with, the medical history: a list of my hospital visits, accidents, broken bones, children, marital status – 'what do you write?' A really difficult moment, of which Wallbrecher was quite unconscious. He noted down: poetry, essays. No mention of any novel. And I wondered what possible use could be made of such information in a patient's file. Wallbrecher said: 'I always admire it when a writer can make a living from his work.' 'So do I,' I replied, though not impertinently, rather on impulse, out of exhaustion, without a moment's thought. Wallbrecher glanced up; he looked irritated. 'I'm quite expensive,' he explained. 'I mean, in comparison to my Italian colleagues, though a discount is possible.'

Why torture myself? The prospect of giving up, there and then, hung in the room and calmed me a little. I was seeing Rome and Rome was to be the place in which I finally abandoned writing. Returning from Wallbrecher to the Villa Massimo, I took a diversion along the Via Aurelia. I was no longer in a hurry and the views over the city and the river were given to me as if in recompense for all those weeks of futile suffering, a ridiculous twist, for sure, but it barely mattered anymore. I walked through Rome and my heart lifted. Again, the spectacle of St Peter's Square, the high dome, then the Piazza del Risorgimento with its equestrian statue, a monument to the 'Arma dei Carabinieri'. The horse looked huge, short-legged, and cumbersome, but it immediately seemed the most sympathetic of all the city's petrified horses, though I had not yet seen the stately statue of Marcus Aurelius, or the Capitoline Square, but that didn't matter anyway, because the horse of the Carabinieri reminded me of my grandfather's last horse, an old mare called Liese, a workhorse I was allowed to sit on as a child, a horse that often came to a complete stop in the midst of her work and only when my grandfather had walked the two kilometres from the farm to the field and whispered something in her ear was she willing to go on. So it is, 'you forget and yield yourself up, say, to the two-fold vision of the crowns of two pines against the honey-coloured sky, and immediately it all comes back, there is meaning again, and form'.[12] I read this much later in Kaschnitz, years too late. And yet, in a way, from that moment on, I was to follow her instructions for living in Rome.

From then on, every so often, I left Massimo Island to explore the city – 'explore' is something of an exaggeration but at least I was out and about, I was *outside* and no longer sitting behind my cupboard. My favourite thing was to accompany our son, Viktor, to his football matches and training sessions. After a successful battle with Italian bureaucracy, my wife had managed to register Viktor at an Italian club. The training ground was located on one of the many bends of the Tiber, close to the Villaggio Olimpico, the 1960s Olympic village: buildings on stilts, with rusty window frames, weather-beaten balconies cluttered with bulky rubbish, the residents' Vespas parked down below. When the wind blew the wrong way, a putrid smell drifted off the river and across the artificial pitches. The matches themselves took place in the most remote places imaginable, places I would never have visited under any other circumstances, places that were neither 'great' nor 'quite great' and certainly not 'magnificent', but for me were close to a revelation, a liberation from the role of Rome-visiting writing Fellow with a genuine interest in art that I had so stubbornly resisted. An unexpected Roman landscape opened to me, one which followed the fixture list of the 'Young Provincials B Team' rather than anything to be found in the guidebooks.

I remember an away game, early one Sunday morning, just off the Via Norma. The playing fields of the Savio football club were on a hillside, surrounded by wire fencing; our route there wound downhill through a very run-down neighbourhood where the tiny houses looked more like bungalows or garages with windows. Walking down the street, we noticed figures of angels on some of the gateposts. There was no one around; everyone was still fast asleep, apart from a little old woman dressed in black. She looked up at us and asked, 'Oggi è domenica?' Is today Sunday? She had just one very large, very broad tooth in her mouth, off to one side, bottom left – or so my notebook tells me.

And, as if off to one side, I had started to write again, something about a wizened old Roman woman and about the sense of complete ease and perfect harmony with the outside world that walk, prior to the match against Savio, had given me: as happens in fairy tales, a passage opens, though this one led not into another world, but into one of my own making. I wrote all this down and it was as if from there, from the Rome of the football playing fields, something was whispering in the ear of the completely petrified workhorse of my writing, at which point it slowly, very slowly, began to move forwards once more.

In the meantime, it had become warmer in Rome, the central heating in the Villa had been turned off, the whistling radiators had fallen silent and the night-time tapping noises had also ceased. My next appointment with Dr Wallbrecher was due. On this occasion, compared to his earlier observations about my writing, the embassy doctor managed to up the ante even further by saying, 'I'm always surprised – writers – that such people still exist!' He did not see any point in examining me and took ninety euros for his fifteen minutes, with no mention of a discount this time. But, by now, I was feeling much better and, almost cheerfully, we said our goodbyes. Also, in the meantime, I had said goodbye to the novel, or more exactly to the novelistic genre. I felt free now to return to my home port of poetry.

One of the highlights of our Roman period was, undoubtedly, the training session which took place the day after the Lazio–Roma derby game: from a distance, during the session, we heard chanting, 'The German, the German, that was the German!', then there was much patting of Viktor's back. Though our son is, strictly speaking, Swedish, he was showered with compliments; as a half-German Swede, he was to be congratulated because of the previous evening's match-winning goal, scored by Miroslav Klose, who had just weeks earlier signed a two-year contract with Lazio. Klose's decisive goal, scored in the final minute of what was the most important game of the season (if not of the Romans' whole lives), also transformed Viktor's position in his team. Though for years, in Berlin and Stockholm, Viktor had only ever played defence or midfield, his coach, Fabrizio, was finally convinced of the qualities of the young Swedish-German as a striker. From that day on, Viktor played up front and nowhere else.

'Is that your father? Is this his car? Is he a writer?' Driving back to the Villa Massimo from the Villaggio Olimpico, we usually also had Niccolò and Nicola in the car, Viktor's Italian football friends from the Swiss school in Rome. Without any inhibitions, using German interspersed with fragments of Italian and Swiss, and as if speaking some kind of secret language that we, the two adults in the distant front seats, were unlikely to be familiar with, they would set about discussing the arcane details of their day-to-day school lives. Mr Massimi, the class teacher, does handstands in class which Nicola finds 'childish' and, in any case, 'not *simpatico*', whereupon Niccolò announces that his father is a scribe as well, writes books, at which point Viktor explains that Oleg's father is a Russian businessman while his mother is an Italian actress which is why a 'driver' – he says 'driver' in English – always picks Oleg up from training, which prompts Nicola to explain what we have already suspected: that their *futbolclub* is the most expensive *scuola calcio* in Rome, more expensive even than the Guardia di Finanza, which obviously says a great deal, at which point Viktor says his classmate, Pietro Paolo Boggio, who plays for De Rossi (a team bankrolled by the professional player, De Rossi), claims their football club was keen to buy him for ninety euros but that he, Pietro Paolo Boggio, was worth at least 110 while others in the team were only being offered thirty or twenty, and so it went on . . .

After every training session, such were the stories that rose from the *ragazzi* in the back seat and it remains a mystery how Pietro the Pro, of all people, arrived at that figure of 110 euros. These days, when I remember Rome, the first thing I see is the five of us in the Volvo, driving through the evening traffic on the Foro Italico: Nicola and Niccolò, Viktor and his mother – two Swedes who had managed to drag a German guy – one who had simply wanted to sit in his room for a year and write – out into the everyday life of Rome. At some point, over dinner, during this period of training sessions and matches played, a question was raised: wouldn't I like to just write a short story, perhaps no more than ten pages or so, on that episode on the Isle of Hiddensee, something I'd always seen as good writing material, and which had originally been intended to be no more than a brief flashback in the now aborted novel?

Those ten pages grew to be five hundred. While I continued, as I did most days, running circuits around Benito Mussolini's park, round the Villa Torlonia, there woke in me a desire to write. Lap after lap, I realised how much the subject matter of the island appealed to me, how it came to meet me, as it were, at a run. But now, I had to take care – no more plans, no three-phase rocket boosters, just notes, sentences, attending, eavesdropping, just squinting and listening to the very source of the novel. Soon, I could see Kruso and Ed standing at the Klausner window, watching the castaways; I saw the 'esskays' – the SKs, *Saisonkräfte*, those historically unique, exotic seasonal workers: philosophers, sociologists, poets, painters, electricians – all trying to live their own independent lives on the island. But I could hardly see myself, though I had been there too, in the summer of 1989, working as a dishwasher in a bar called the Klausner on the rocky coast of Hiddensee.

Then, on one of my Torlonia laps (I can see, from my notebook, this was on 27 May 2011), the image of the Soviet general came to me for the first time, a Russian general standing on the edge of the Baltic Sea, Kruso's father coming to take his son home. Even in that first vision or image of him, the general appeared as a kind of *deus ex machina*, his powerful presence – a tall man with his coat unbuttoned and an armoured cruiser in the background – appealed to me tremendously, at once familiar and, at the same time, strange enough to herald the end of an epoch. Familiar because it corresponded both to my own experience in military service and to the iconography of the comrade-in-arms, our own 'big brother' and our most important ally, bound in steadfast friendship, as we had always been told. Yet I was still nervous and had committed hardly anything to paper – I was waiting. I realised what was missing from this image less than a week later, during an open-air concert in the Villino of the Villa Massimo. At one particular moment, as the musician played his saxophone, he was positioned against the backdrop of an aeroplane crossing the sky, an Air Berlin plane preparing to land at Ciampino Airport (the Villa lay under the flight path). And, at that moment, there was an extraordinary interleaving of sounds: the familiar tumult of the city of Rome, of noise versus art which I knew well enough, and I almost laughed out loud in the middle of the concert, not because of the Air Berlin plane, but with delight at my new general, for in that moment suddenly his trouser legs were wet. A little limp Baltic wave had risen up and splashed his trouser legs. And there he was, standing in the fullness of his power, broken now in so many ways. It was an image that immediately encompassed the whole story, an image I felt I could trust without reservation, a doorway through which I would be able to pass, into the material of that time.

To create the image of the general, what was needed, to begin with, was that I set aside my own experiences. I had to become more detached from the historical sources that, in my first efforts, had so overwhelmed me with detail, moments of interest and superfluous information. The image of the general was incomparably more pertinent than any of my earlier research or reflection, its ambient value matching precisely what was to be reconstructed, not in the sense of any factual reality or verifiable historical truth, but in the sense of the story of a time long gone that demanded to be told. A huge number of disparate memories and emotions were gathered within it (in this vision of the general with his soggy trouser legs). The image functioned as a refuge, it was a storehouse of compacted time, at the least a honeycomb for my writing. And more than that: it was as if I had actually remembered it, it had that underlying feeling of narrative truth, as if I really did recall seeing the general standing beside the Baltic Sea in the autumn of 1989.

'How can the past increase when it no longer exists?' asks St Augustine in his *Confessions* and he goes on: 'It can only be that the mind, which regulates this process, performs three functions, those of expectation, attention and memory. The future, which it expects, passes through the present, to which it attends, into the past, which it remembers.'[13] As I have said, my ten pages grew to become five hundred. An expansion that makes it possible for me here to recall my novel's early Roman history – a tale of crisis and panic and ridiculousness, yet also, as Kaschnitz once described the experience of living in Rome, 'a fragment of a new birth, vulnerability, nakedness'.[14]

(2016, 2020)

NOTES

1   Jürgen Becker, 'Against the Conservation of the Literary Status Quo' ('Gegen die Erhaltung des literarischen Status Quo'), presented at the Berliner Kritiker-Colloquium 1963, published in 1964.

2   Translation by Martyn Crucefix of the whole of the poem 'müde bin ich' in Lutz Seiler's collection *pech & blende*, a collection published by And Other Stories in 2023 as *Pitch & Glint* in Stefan Tobler's translation.

3   Catherine Caufield, *Multiple Exposures: Chronicles of the Radiation Age* (HarperCollins, 1989).

4   Translation by Martyn Crucefix of part of the poem 'gravitation' ('gravity') in Lutz Seiler's collection *pech & blende* (*Pitch & Glint*).

5   Cees Nooteboom, 'The Secret in the White Around the Words' in *Minima Poetica: Für eine Poetik des zeitgenössischen Gedichts*, ed. Joachim Sartorius (Kiepenheuer & Witsch, 1999).

6   Paul Bowles, interviewed by Peter Henning, published as 'Absprung ins Nichts' in *Die Welt*, 19 November 1999.

7   Translation by Martyn Crucefix of the whole of the poem 'sonntags dachte ich an gott' in Lutz Seiler's collection *pech & blende* (*Pitch & Glint*).

8   Gaston Bachelard, 'My Lamp and My Blank Paper', the epilogue to *The Flame of a Candle* (*La Flamme d'une chandelle*, Les Presses universitaires de France, 1961).

9   Marie Luise Kaschnitz, *The Bridge of Angels: Roman Reflections* (*Engelsbrücke: Römische Betrachtungen*, Claassen, 1955).

10 Marie Luise Kaschnitz, 'The Work of Art' ('Das Kunstwerk'), in *Collected Works*, vol. 7 (Suhrkamp, 1989).

11 Marie Luise Kaschnitz, *Places* (*Orte*, Insel, 1975).

12 Marie Luise Kaschnitz, *The Bridge of Angels: Roman Reflections.*
13 St Augustine, *The Confessions.*
14 Marie Luise Kaschnitz, *The Bridge of Angels: Roman Reflections.*

EDITORIAL NOTE

SOURCES FOR THE GERMAN TEXTS

Unless otherwise stated, all the texts in *In Case of Loss* are taken and translated from Lutz Seiler's essay collection *Sonntags dachte ich an Gott*, Suhrkamp Verlag, 2004.

'The Tired Territory' is an essay that originally appeared in the collection *Sonntags dachte ich an Gott* as 'Heimaten', and then in a new version entitled 'Das Territorium der Müdigkeit' in his University of Heidelberg poetics lectures *Laubsäge und Scheinbrücke: Aus der Vorgeschichte des Schreibens*, Universitätsverlag Winter GmbH Heidelberg, 2020.

'The Soggy Hems of His Soviet Trousers' was published in a first German version as 'Von Rom nach Hiddensee' in *Die römische Saison*, Topalian & Milani Verlag, 2016, and then in a reworked version entitled '"Die nassen Ränder seiner sowjetischen Hosenbeine" – Eingangsbilder ins Erzählen vergangener Zeit' in *Laubsäge und Scheinbrücke*. Under Lutz Seiler's guidance, the English translation of the two essays is a revised version of the text of the later poetics lectures published in *Laubsäge und Scheinbrücke*.

'The Invocation' first appeared in *Akzente. Zeitschrift für Literatur*, issue 3 of 2005, entitled 'Schönheit', and was then published in book form as *Die Anrufung*, Ulrich Keicher Verlag, 2005, and in *Turksib*, Suhrkamp Verlag, 2008.

'In the Movie Bunker' was first published in *Archiv verworfener Möglichkeiten Fotos und Texte* by Naomi Schenck, 2010, and in an expanded version in *Im Kinobunker*, Ulrich Keicher Verlag, 2012, before becoming part of Seiler's non-fiction collection *Am Kap des guten Abends*, Insel Verlag, 2018, from which revised version this translation has been made.

'The Flute Player' first appeared in *Du: die Zeitschrift der Kultur*, volume 66, 2006, and was subsequently published in *Am Kap des guten Abends*.

PREVIOUS PUBLICATIONS IN ENGLISH

Thanks to *PN Review* for publishing 'Babelsberg: Brief Thoughts on Ernst Meister', 'In the Anchor Jar' and 'The Flute Player' in number 270, March–April 2023, and to *Granta* for publishing 'In the Movie Bunker' in issue 165, November 2023.

Dear readers,

As well as relying on bookshop sales, And Other Stories relies on subscriptions from people like you for many of our books, whose stories other publishers often consider too risky to take on.

Our subscribers don't just make the books physically happen. They also help us approach booksellers, because we can demonstrate that our books already have readers and fans. And they give us the security to publish in line with our values, which are collaborative, imaginative and 'shamelessly literary'.

All of our subscribers:

- receive a first-edition copy of each of the books they subscribe to
- are thanked by name at the end of our subscriber-supported books
- receive little extras from us by way of thank you, for example: postcards created by our authors

BECOME A SUBSCRIBER,
OR GIVE A SUBSCRIPTION TO A FRIEND

Visit andotherstories.org/subscriptions to help make our books happen. You can subscribe to books we're in the process of making. To purchase books we have already published, we urge you to support your local or favourite bookshop and order directly from them – the often unsung heroes of publishing.

OTHER WAYS TO GET INVOLVED

If you'd like to know about upcoming events and reading groups (our foreign-language reading groups help us choose books to publish, for example) you can:

- join our mailing list at: andotherstories.org
- follow us on Twitter: @andothertweets
- join us on Facebook: facebook.com/AndOtherStoriesBooks
- admire our books on Instagram: @andotherpics
- follow our blog: andotherstories.org/ampersand

THIS BOOK WAS MADE POSSIBLE
THANKS TO THE SUPPORT OF

Aaron Bogner
Aaron McEnery
Aaron Schneider
Abbie Bambridge
Abigail Charlesworth
Abigail Gambrill
Abigail Walton
Adam Lenson
Ajay Sharma
Al Ullman
Alan McMonagle
Alasdair Cross
Alastair Gillespie
Albert Puente
Alec Logan
Aleksi Rennes
Alex Fleming
Alex Liebman
Alex Pearce
Alex Pheby
Alex Ramsey
Alexander Bunin
Alexandra Kay-Wallace
Alexandra Stewart
Alexandra Tammaro
Alexandra Webb
Alfred Tobler
Ali Ersahin
Ali Riley
Ali Smith
Ali Usman
Alia Carter
Alison Hardy
Alison Lock
Aliya Rashid
Alyssa Rinaldi
Alyssa Tauber
Amado Floresca
Amaia Gabantxo
Amanda
Amanda Fisher
Amanda Read
Amelia Dowe

Amine Hamadache
Amitav Hajra
Amos Hintermann
Amy and Jamie
Amy Benson
Amy Bojang
Amy Hatch
Amy Tabb
Ana Novak
Andrea Barlien
Andrea Oyarzabal
    Koppes
Andreas Zbinden
Andrew Kerr-Jarrett
Andrew Lahy
Andrew Marston
Andrew Martino
Andrew McCallum
Andrew Place
Andrew Rego
Andrew Wright
Andrzej Walzchojnacki
Andy Corsham
Andy Marshall
Angela Joyce
Angelina Izzo
Angus Walker
Ann Morgan
Anna Finneran
Anna French
Anna Hawthorne
Anna Milsom
Anna Zaranko
Anne Edyvean
Anne Frost
Anne Germanacos
Anne-Marie Renshaw
Anne Ryden
Anne Willborn
Anne Withane
Annette Volger
Annie McDermott
Anonymous

Anthony Cotton
Anthony Fortenberry
Anthony Quinn
Antonia Lloyd-Jones
Antonia Saske
Antony Pearce
Aoibheann McCann
April Hernandez
Arathi Devandran
Archie Davies
Aron Trauring
Asako Serizawa
Ashleigh Phillips
Ashley Marshall
Audrey Holmes
Audrey Mash
Audrey Small
Aurelia Wills
Barbara Mellor
Barbara Spicer
Barry John Fletcher
Barry Norton
Beatrice Taylor
Becky Cherriman
Becky Matthewson
Ben Buchwald
Ben Schofield
Ben Thornton
Ben Walter
Benjamin Judge
Benjamin Pester
Beth Heim de Bera
Betty Roberts
Bianca Jackson
Bianca Winter
Bill Fletcher
Billy-Ray Belcourt
Bjørnar Djupevik Hagen
Blazej Jedras
Brandon Clar
Brenda Wrobel
Brendan Dunne
Briallen Hopper

Brian Anderson
Brian Byrne
Brian Callaghan
Brian Isabelle
Brian Smith
Briana Sprague
Brianna Soloski
Bridget Maddison
Bridget Prentice
Brooks Williams
Buck Johnston & Camp
  Bosworth
Burkhard Fehsenfeld
Caitlin Halpern
Callie Steven
Cameron Adams
Camilla Imperiali
Carla Castanos
Carole Hardy
Carole Parkhouse
Carolina Pineiro
Caroline Kim
Caroline Lodge
Caroline Perry
Caroline West
Carolyn Carter
Carolyn A Schroeder
Catharine Braithwaite
Catherine Campbell
Catherine Cleary
Catherine Lambert
Catherine Tandy
Catherine Williamson
Cathryn Siegal-Bergman
Cathy Galvin
Cathy Sowell
Catie Kosinski
Cecilia Rossi
Cecilia Uribe
Cerileigh Guichelaar
Chandler Sanchez
Charlene Huggins
Charles Fernyhough
Charles Kovach
Charles Dee Mitchell
Charles Rowe
Charles Wats

Charlie Levin
Charlie Small
Charlotte Coulthard
Charlotte Furness
Charlotte Holtam
Charlotte Ryland
Charlotte Whittle
Chenxin Jiang
China Miéville
Chris Burton
Chris Gribble
Chris Johnstone
Chris Potts
Chris Senior
Chris Stergalas
Chris Stevenson
Christian Schuhmann
Christiana Spens
Christine Elliott
Christopher Fox
Christopher Stout
Chuck Woodman
Claire Adams
Claire Brooksby
Clare Wilkins
Claudia Mazzoncini
Clifford Wright
Clíona Quigley
Colin Denyer
Colin Hewlett
Colin Matthews
Collin Brooke
Conor McMeel
Courtney Lilly
Craig Kennedy
Cynthia De La Torre
Cyrus Massoudi
Daisy Savage
Dale Wisely
Damon Copeland
Dan Vigliano
Daniel Axelbaum
Daniel Cossai
Daniel Coxon
Daniel Gillespie
Daniel Hahn
Daniel Hayes

Daniel Sanford
Daniel Smith
Daniel Stewart
Daniel Syrovy
Daniela Steierberg
Darcie Vigliano
Darren Boyling
Darren Gillen
Darren Wapplington
Darryll Rogers
Dave Lander
David Anderson
David Ball
David Cowan
David Gould
David Greenlaw
David Gunnarsson
David Hebblethwaite
David Higgins
David Johnson-Davies
David Miller
David Richardson
David Shriver
David Smith
David Smith
David Wacks
David F Long
Dawn Bass
Dean Taucher
Deb Unferth
Debbie Pinfold
Deborah Green
Deborah McLean
Declan O'Driscoll
Delaina Haslam
Denis Larose
Derek Sims
Devin Day
Diane Hamilton
Dietrich Menzel
Dinesh Prasad
Dirk Hanson
Domenica Devine
Dominic Bailey
Dominic Nolan
Dominick Santa
  Cattarina

Dominique Brocard
Dominique Hudson
Dornith Doherty
Dorothy Bottrell
Dugald Mackie
Duncan Chambers
Duncan Clubb
Duncan Macgregor
Dustin Chase-Woods
Dustin Haviv
Dyanne Prinsen
Earl James
Ebba Tornérhielm
Ed Smith
Edward Champion
Ekaterina Beliakova
Elaine Rodrigues
Eleanor Maier
Elif Aganoglu
Elina Zicmane
Elizabeth Braswell
Elizabeth Coombes
Elizabeth Draper
Elizabeth Franz
Elizabeth Guss
Elizabeth Leach
Elizabeth Seals
Elizabeth Sieminski
Elizabeth Wood
Ella Sabiduria
Ellen Beardsworth
Ellie Goddard
Ellie Small
Emiliano Gomez
Emily Gladhart
Emma Biclecki
Emma Louise Grove
Emma Post
Emma Teale
Eric Weinstock
Erin Cameron Allen
Erin Feeley
Erin Louttit
Ethan Madarieta
Ethan White
Evelyn Eldridge
Evelyn Reis

Ewan Tant
Fawzia Kane
Fay Barrett
Faye Williams
Felicity Le Quesne
Felix Valdivieso
Finbarr Farragher
Finn Brocklesby
Fiona Liddle
Fiona Mozley
Fiona Quinn
Fiona Wilson
Fran Sanderson
Frances Dinger
Frances Harvey
Frances Thiessen
Francesca Hemery
Francesca Sanderson
Frank Curtis
Frank Pearson
Frank Rodrigues
Frank van Orsouw
Freddie Radford
Gail Marten
Gala Copley
Gavin Aitchison
Gavin Collins
Gawain Espley
Gemma Bird
Geoff Thrower
Geoffrey Cohen
Geoffrey Urland
George McCaig
George Stanbury
George Wilkinson
Georgia Panteli
Georgia Shomidie
Georgina Hildick-Smith
Georgina Norton
Geraldine Brodie
Gerry Craddock
Gill Boag-Munroe
Gillian Grant
Gillian Stern
Gina Filo
Gina Heathcote
Glen Bornais

Glenn Russell
Gloria Gunn
Gordon Cameron
Gosia Pennar
Grace Payne
Graham Blenkinsop
Graham R Foster
Grant Ray-Howett
Gregor von dem
 Knesebeck
Hadil Balzan
Halina Schiffman-Shilo
Hannah Freeman
Hannah Harford-Wright
Hannah Rapley
Hannah Jane
 Lownsbrough
Hans Lazda
Harriet Stiles
Haydon Spenceley
Heidi James
Helen Berry
Henrietta Dunsmuir
Henrike Laehnemann
Hilary Munro
Holly Down
Howard Robinson
Hyoung-Won Park
Ian Betteridge
Ian McMillan
Ian Mond
Ian Randall
Ida Grochowska
Imogen Clarke
Ines Alfano
Ingrid Peterson
Irene Mansfield
Irina Tzanova
Isabella Garment
Isabella Weibrecht
Isobel Dixon
Ivy Lin
J Drew Hancock-Teed
Jack Brown
Jacob Musser
Jacqueline Haskell
Jacqueline Lademann

Jacqueline Vint
Jacquelynn Williams
Jake Baldwinson
James Avery
James Beck
James Crossley
James Cubbon
James Higgs
James Leonard
James Lesniak
James Portlock
James Ruland
James Scudamore
James Silvestro
Jan Hicks
Jane Dolman
Jane Roberts
Jane Roberts
Jane Woollard
Janet Digby
Janis Carpenter
Janna Eastwood
Jasmine Gideon
Jason Bell
Jason Lever
Jason Montano
Jason Timermanis
Jason Whalley
Jayne Watson
JE Crispin
Jeanne Guyon
Jeff Collins
Jeff Fesperman
Jen Calleja
Jen Hardwicke
Jenifer Logie
Jennifer Fain
Jennifer Fosket
Jennifer Mills
Jennifer Watts
Jennifer Yanoschak
Jenny Huth
Jenny McNally
Jeremy Koenig
Jeremy Sabol
Jerome Mersky
Jess Wood

Jesse Coleman
Jessica Gately
Jessica Kibler
Jessica Laine
Jessica Queree
Jethro Soutar
Joan Dowgin
Joanna Luloff
Joao Pedro Bragatti
  Winckler
JoDee Brandon
Jodie Adams
Joe Huggins
Joel Swerdlow
Joelle Young
Johannes Menzel
Johannes Georg Zipp
John Bennett
John Berube
John Bogg
John Conway
John Gent
John Hodgson
John Kelly
John McWhirter
John Purser
John Reid
John Shadduck
John Shaw
John Steigerwald
John Walsh
John Whiteside
John Winkelman
John Wyatt
Jolene Smith
Jon Riches
Jonas House
Jonathan Blaney
Jonathan Fiedler
Jonathan Gharraie
Jonathan Harris
Jonathan Huston
Joni Chan
Jonny Kiehlmann
Jordana Carlin
Jorid Martinsen
Joseph Thomas

Josh Sumner
Joshua Briggs
Joshua Davis
Joy Paul
Judith Gruet-Kaye
Julia Foden
Julia Rochester
Julia Sutton-Mattocks
Julia Von Dem Knesebeck
Julian Hemming
Julie Greenwalt
Juliet Swann
Junius Hoffman
Jupiter Jones
Juraj Janik
Justine Sherwood
Kaarina Hollo
Kaelyn Davis
Kaja R Anker-Rasch
Kalina Rose
Kamaryn Norris
Karen Gilbert
Karin Mckercher
Katarina Dzurekova
Katarzyna Bartoszynska
Kate Beswick
Kate Carlton-Reditt
Kate Shires
Kate Stein
Katharine Robbins
Katherine Sotejeff-
  Wilson
Kathleen McLean
Kathrin Zander
Kathryn Burruss
Kathryn Edwards
Kathryn Williams
Katia Wengraf
Katie Brown
Katie Cooke
Katie Freeman
Katie Grant
Katy Robinson
Kavitha Buggana
Kay Cunningham
Keith Walker
Kelly Hydrick

Ken Geniza
Kenneth Blythe
Kenneth Masloski
Kenneth Peabody
Kent Curry
Kent McKernan
Kerry Parke
Kevin Winter
Kieran Rollin
Kieron James
Kim Streets
Kirsten Hey
KL Ee
Kris Ann Trimis
Kristen Tcherneshoff
Kristen Tracey
Kristin Djuve
Kristy Richardson
Krystale Tremblay-Moll
Krystine Phelps
Kurt Navratil
Kyle Pienaar
Kyra Wilder
Lacy Wolfe
Lana Selby
Lara Vergnaud
Laura Murphy
Laura Pugh
Laura Rangeley
Laura Zlatos
Lauren Pout
Lauren Rea
Lauren Rosenfield
Laurence Laluyaux
Lee Harbour
Leona Iosifidou
Liliana Lobato
Lilie Weaver
Lily Blacksell
Lily Robert-Foley
Linda Jones
Linda Lewis
Linda Milam
Linda Whittle
Lindsay Brammer
Lindsey Ford
Lisa Dillman

Lisa Leahigh
Lisa Simpson
Liz Clifford
Liz Ketch
Liz Wilding
Lorna Bleach
Lottie Smith
Louise Evans
Louise Greenberg
Louise Jolliffe
Louise Smith
Lucie Taylor
Lucinda Smith
Lucy Moffatt
Luiz Cesar Peres
Luke Healey
Luke Murphy
Lyndia Thomas
Lynn Fung
Lynn Grant
Lynn Martin
Madden Aleia
Madison Taylor-Hayden
Maeve Lambe
Maggie Livesey
Malgorzata Rokicka
Mandy Wight
Marco Medjimorec
Margaret Jull Costa
Margaret Wood
Mari-Liis Calloway
Maria Ahnhem Farrar
María Lomunno
Maria Losada
Marie Cloutier
Marina Castledine
Marion Pennicuik
Marja S Laaksonen
Mark Bridgman
Mark Reynolds
Mark Sargent
Mark Sheets
Mark Sztyber
Mark Tronco
Mark Troop
Mark Waters
Martha W Hood

Martin Brown
Martin Price
Martin Eric Rodgers
Mary Addonizio
Mary Clarke
Mary Heiss
Mary Wang
Maryse Meijer
Mathias Ruthner
Mathieu Trudeau
Matt Davies
Matt Greene
Matthew Cooke
Matthew Crossan
Matthew Eatough
Matthew Francis
Matthew Gill
Matthew Lowe
Matthew Woodman
Matthias Rosenberg
Maureen and Bill Wright
Max Cairnduff
Max Longman
Maxwell Mankoff
Maya Feile Tomes
Meaghan Delahunt
Meg Lovelock
Megan Wittling
Mei-Ting Belle Huang
Mel Pryor
Melanie Stray
Melissa Beck
Melissa Stogsdill
Melynda Nuss
Michael Aguilar
Michael Bichko
Michael Bittner
Michael Boog
Michael James Eastwood
Michael Floyd
Michael Gavin
Michael Schneiderman
Michele Whitfeld
Michelle Mercaldo
Michelle Mirabella
Miguel Head
Mike Abram

Mike Schneider
Miles Smith-Morris
Mme Vita Osborne
Moira Weir
Molly Foster
Mona Arshi
Morayma Jimenez
Morgan Lyons
Moriah Haefner
MP Boardman
Nancy Garruba
Nancy Jacobson
Nancy Langfeldt
Nancy Oakes
Naomi Morauf
Nargis McCarthy
Nasiera Foflonker
Natalie Ricks
Nathalie Teitler
Nathan McNamara
Nathan Weida
Niamh Thompson
Nichola Smalley
Nicholas Brown
Nicholas Rutherford
Nick Chapman
Nick James
Nick Marshall
Nick Nelson & Rachel
Eley
Nick Sidwell
Nick Twemlow
Nicola Cook
Nicola Hart
Nicola Mira
Nicola Sandiford
Nicolas Sampson
Nicole Matteini
Nigel Fishburn
Niki Sammut
Nina Todorova
Noah Brumfield
Norma Gillespie
Norman Batchelor
Norman Carter
Norman Nehmetallah
Invisible Publishing

Odilia Corneth
Olga Zilberbourg
Olivia Clarke
Olivia Powers
Olivia Scott
Olivia Spring
Paavan Buddhdev
Pamela Ritchie
Pamela Tao
Pankaj Mishra
Pat Winslow
Patricia Beesley
Patricia Gurton
Patrick Hawley
Patrick King
Paul Bangert
Paul Cray
Paul Ewing
Paul Jones
Paul Munday
Paul Myatt
Paul Nightingale
Paul Scott
Paul Segal
Pavlos Stavropoulos
Pearse Devlin
Penelope Hewett-Brown
Peter and Nancy Ffitch
Peter Gaukrodger
Peter Griffin
Peter Hayden
Peter McCambridge
Peter Rowland
Peter Wells
Petra Hendrickson
Petra Stapp
Phil Bartlett
Phil Curry
Philip Herbert
Philip Nulty
Philip Warren
Philip Williams
Phillipa Clements
Phoebe Millerwhite
Phyllis Reeve
Piet Van Bockstal
Rachael de Moravia

Rachael Williams
Rachel Adducci
Rachel Andrews
Rachel Beddow
Rachel Belt
Rachel Carter
Rachel Darnley-Smith
Rachel Van Riel
Rahul Kanakia
Ralph Cowling
Ralph Jacobowitz
Raminta Uselytė
Ramona Pulsford
Ramya Purkanti
Rebecca Caldwell
Rebecca Carter
Rebecca Maddox
Rebecca Marriott
Rebecca Michel
Rebecca Moss
Rebecca O'Reilly
Rebecca Peer
Rebecca Shaak
Rebecca Starks
Rebecca Surin
Rebekka Bremmer
Renee Otmar
Renee Thomas
Rhiannon Armstrong
Rich Sutherland
Richard Ellis
Richard Gwyn
Richard Mansell
Richard Santos
Richard Shea
Richard Soundy
Richard Village
Rishi Dastidar
Rita Kaar
Rita Marrinson
Rita O'Brien
Robert Gillett
Robert Hamilton
Robert Hannah
Robert Sliman
Robert Weeks
Robin McLean

Robin Taylor
Robina Frank
Rodrigo Alvarez
Roger Ramsden
Ronan O'Shea
Rory Williamson
Rosalind May
Rosalind Ramsay
Rose Crichton
Rosemary Horsewood
Rosie Sparrowhawk
Royston Tester
Roz Simpson
Rupert Ziziros
Ruth Edgar
Ryan Day
Ryan Oliver
Ryan Pierce
Sally Baker
Sally Warner
Sam Gordon
Samuel Crosby
Sara Bea
Sara Kittleson
Sara Unwin
Sarah Arboleda
Sarah Brewer
Sarah Lucas
Sarah Pybus
Scott Chiddister
Scott Russell
Sean Johnston
Sean Kottke
Sean McGivern
Selina Guinness
Serena Brett
Severijn Hagemeijer
Shannon Knapp
Sharon Dilworth
Sharon McCammon
Shauna Gilligan
Sian Hannah
Sienna Kang
Simak Ali
Simon James
Simon Malcolm
Simon Pitney

Simon Robertson
Siriol Hugh-Jones
SK Grout
ST Dabbagh
Stacy Rodgers
Stefano Mula
Stephan Eggum
Stephanie De Los Santos
Stephanie Miller
Stephanie Smee
Stephanie Wasek
Stephen Cowley
Stephen Fuller
Stephen Pearsall
Stephen Yates
Steve Chapman
Steve Clough
Steve Dearden
Steve Tuffnell
Steven Norton
Stewart Eastham
Stu Hennigan
Stuart Grey
Stuart & Sarah Quinn
Stuart Wilkinson
Sunny Payson
Susan Edsall
Susan Jaken
Susan Wachowski
Susan Winter
Suzanne and Nick Davies
Suzanne Kirkham
Sylvie Zannier-Betts
Tallulah Fairfax
Tania Hershman
Tara Roman
Tatiana Griffin
Teresa Werner
Tess Cohen
Tess Lewis
Tessa Lang
Theo Voortman
Thom Keep
Thomas Alt
Thomas Campbell
Thomas van den Bout
Tiffany Lehr

Tim Kelly
Tim Nicholls
Tim Scott
Timothy Moffatt
Tina Rotherham-
   Winqvist
Tina Juul Møller
Toby Halsey
Toby Ryan
Tom Darby
Tom Doyle
Tom Franklin
Tom Gray
Tom McAllister
Tom Stafford
Tom Whatmore
Tracy Birch
Tracy Northup
Trent Leleu
Trevor Latimer
Trevor Wald
Turner Docherty
Val & Tom Flechtner
Valerie O'Riordan
Vanessa Fernandez
   Greene
Vanessa Heggie
Vanessa Nolan
Veronika Haacker
   Lukacs
Victor Meadowcroft
Victor Saouma
Victoria Goodbody
Victoria Huggins
Vijay Pattisapu
Vikki O'Neill
Wendy Call
Wendy Langridge
Will Herbert
Will Weir
William Leibovici
William Mackenzie
William Orton
Yana Ellis
Yoora Yi Tenen
Zachary Maricondia
Zoë Brasier